T5-AFC-887
SEATTLE
The Time Has Come
Frederick & Nelson
WILLIAM STINE
Frederick & Nelson

◆ © JIM CORWIN

SEATTLE

The Time Has Come

Introduction
Erik Lacitis

Art Direction
Bob Kimball

URBAN
TAPESTRY
SERIES
TOWERY
PUBLISHING, INC.

SEATTLE
The Time Has Come

It was the middle of summer, during one of the 58 days a year in Seattle that are totally cloudless. Everything was perfect. The temperature was in the high 70s, there was the gentlest of breezes and nary a speck of smog, and, in the last hour, Bill Gates had just earned another $1 million, give or take a few hundred thousand, depending on Nasdaq's whims.

There was a mix of us locals and tourists on the charter fishing boat, trolling for salmon, a 12-pound silver already having been caught and stored in the cooler. We were on Elliott Bay, right in front of downtown Seattle, and we couldn't help it—we had to pause to savor the magnificent moment.

Our gaze could sweep across the panoramic view of the Space Needle, the skyscrapers, the industrial cranes on the working waterfront, the ferries that carry 25 million commuters a year, and—hovering in the background—our very own snow-clad Mount Rainier, the (hopefully) dormant volcano that has served as a backdrop for countless photos.

No matter how many times you've seen the view, no matter how far back you can trace your Pacific Northwest ancestry, such a setting still makes you pause in wonder. And here we were, fishing for salmon right in front of a bustling downtown! Where else could you do that!

I mean, we were just a few minutes' boat ride from sipping a microbrew at a waterfront lounge. We weren't in some forsaken outpost that was 10 hours away. From the boat, you could take out the cell phone and talk to a buddy in one of the office buildings. You could wave at him, and, if he had binoculars, he could see you. One of the tourists said it for all of us: It doesn't get better than this. The tourist was already talking about moving here. ▶

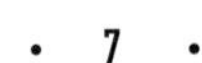

40-23

33
USA
Jumbo Jets
1999

We've gotten used to the accolades and being placed in those "best of" lists—more than 40 such rankings in the past decade, from being among the most family-friendly cities to being the number one best place for doing business to being the healthiest city for women.

We locals are proud, but at the same time we worry. There has been a seismic change in our economy. The region now boasts 10,000 millionaires, and a good portion of them gained their wealth from the software industry that emerged in the 1980s.

Seattle began as a lumber town and moved on to become a supply outpost for all the thousands of hopefuls trekking to Alaska for Yukon gold. Next, it became a center for shipbuilding, and then, with World War II and the Boeing Company, became the site for mass-producing B-17 and B-29 bombers. In 1954, Boeing began manufacturing the 707, marking the beginning of mass air travel.

Boeing is still the major employer in the region with a payroll of nearly $6 billion for its 110,000 workers here. The economic fortunes of the company also have been those of the city. When Boeing had massive layoffs in the early 1970s, there appeared the infamous billboard, "Will the last person leaving Seattle turn out the lights?"

Then, in the 1980s, Microsoft arrived, founded by two local sons, Bill Gates and Paul Allen. One of the first computer-programming efforts by Gates was when he was a student at Lakeside School in Seattle in the late 1960s, and he secretly changed the class-scheduling program so he'd be about the only guy in a class full of girls.

Gates is now the richest man in the world, worth $60 billion, according to *Forbes* magazine's annual ranking. Allen, who quit Microsoft after being diagnosed with Hodgkin's disease (a battle he fought and won), is worth $28 billion. To put their wealth in perspective, in 1997, it's estimated these two paid more than $1 billion simply on capital gains taxes from selling Microsoft stock.

What shocks even the locals is this other statistic: The software industry here employs less than a fifth of Boeing's workforce. But that same software workforce actually earns more annually, a staggering $6.8 billion, including stock options. One estimate puts the average software wage in the county at $401,000 a year.

You bet it has been a seismic change. ▶

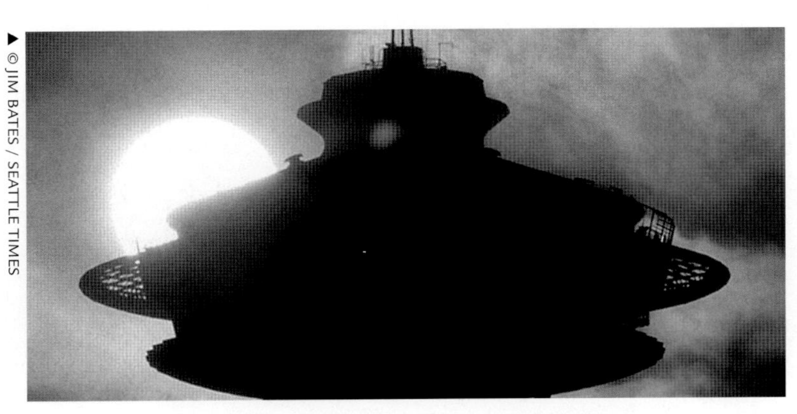

▶ © JIM BATES / SEATTLE TIMES

For one thing, the newly rich techies have been buying and building themselves very expensive homes. In 1990, the million-dollar home sales in the county numbered a total of 42. Nine years later, that number had shot to 384. It also has changed the dynamics of what used to be middle-class neighborhoods such as Wallingford, where I grew up, and where a typical three-bedroom frame house is listed at $300,000 or $400,000.

All of this has left many in Seattle wondering what has happened to the city's soul. What happened to the Seattle in which the really big deal was hosting the Century 21 World's Fair in 1962, or the annual Seafair parade with those garrulous guys dressed up as pirates, scaring the heck out of the little kids? We were just a big little town then, tucked in a corner of America. I remember visiting New York City in the 1970s, and being asked in all seriousness if we got all the network TV channels here.

We have always, I think, been stubbornly proud of our outdoorsy, isolated, rainy heritage. One time, I read to some elementary-school kids the initial impressions of the first white settlers who made their way here. It was a rainy dawn on November 13, 1851, and 10 adults and 12 children landed on what is now Alki Beach in West Seattle. What they found waiting was a roofless log cabin. One of the women who stayed on the boat later remembered that typically drizzly autumn day: "[W]hen the women got into the rowboat to go ashore they were crying every one of 'em. . . . The last glimpse I had of them was the women standing under the trees with their wet sun bonnets all lopping down over their faces and their aprons to their eyes." ▶

▲ © JIMI LOTT / SEATTLE TIMES

The kids nodded. Yeah, the rain, the stuff that on winter days greets them when they wake up, and after school drenches the soccer fields where they practice. The visitor's bureau likes to point out that the annual rainfall here is 36 inches—less than New York City, Atlanta, or Boston, for example. Maybe, but the locals know the truth about our Novembers, Decembers, Januaries, Februaries, and usually a few other months—always cloudy, always a drizzle.

Tom Robbins, the Northwest author of *Even Cowgirls Get the Blues*, wrote about the rain, "In the deepest, darkest heart of winter, when the sky resembles bad banana baby food for months on end . . . I grow happier with each fresh storm . . . 'What's so hot about the sun?' I ask. Sunbeams are a lot like tourists: intruding where they don't belong. . . . Raindrops, on the other hand, introverted, feral, buddhistically cool, behave as if they live here. Which, of course, they do."

In that first batch of white settlers 150 years ago were such families as the Dennys and the Borens, after whom now are named Seattle streets and buildings. They determinedly set about building themselves a city, deciding a good place to start was along the Elliott Bay waterfront, as it was deep enough for a harbor for shipping out timber.

The first logs were cut from what is now the nearby Beacon Hill neighborhood. The term "skid row" originated here when loggers built wood skids to move logs down to the waterfront. The skids would become the separation from the more respectable downtown and the whorehouses and booze joints to the south. Seattle then was a hell-raising place.

Two decades ago, I had the chance to interview the late Bill Speidel, a local historian who, admittedly, tended to romanticize the yesteryears.

It frustrated Speidel that modern Seattle had (and still does have) a reputation for Scandinavian reservedness, all polite and orderly. The Swedes, Norwegians, and Danes immigrated here in the 1900s to work in the sawmills and in the fishing fleets. Many settled north of downtown in Ballard, which once was its own city before being annexed.

Speidel told me about those early days: "See, Seattle has always had a split personality—the swingers and the Christers. I did some checking, and I figured out some statistics for this city in 1892. Do you know that 87 percent of the city budget was paid for by gambling, prostitution, and liquor? I guess the swinging got a little too far, because then, in 1907, we got the blue laws that made illegal anything that was fun. We've spent the last 70 years trying to recover from those laws. We behave something like when you visit a maiden aunt. You watch your language." ▶

▶ © MICHAEL TOWNSEND

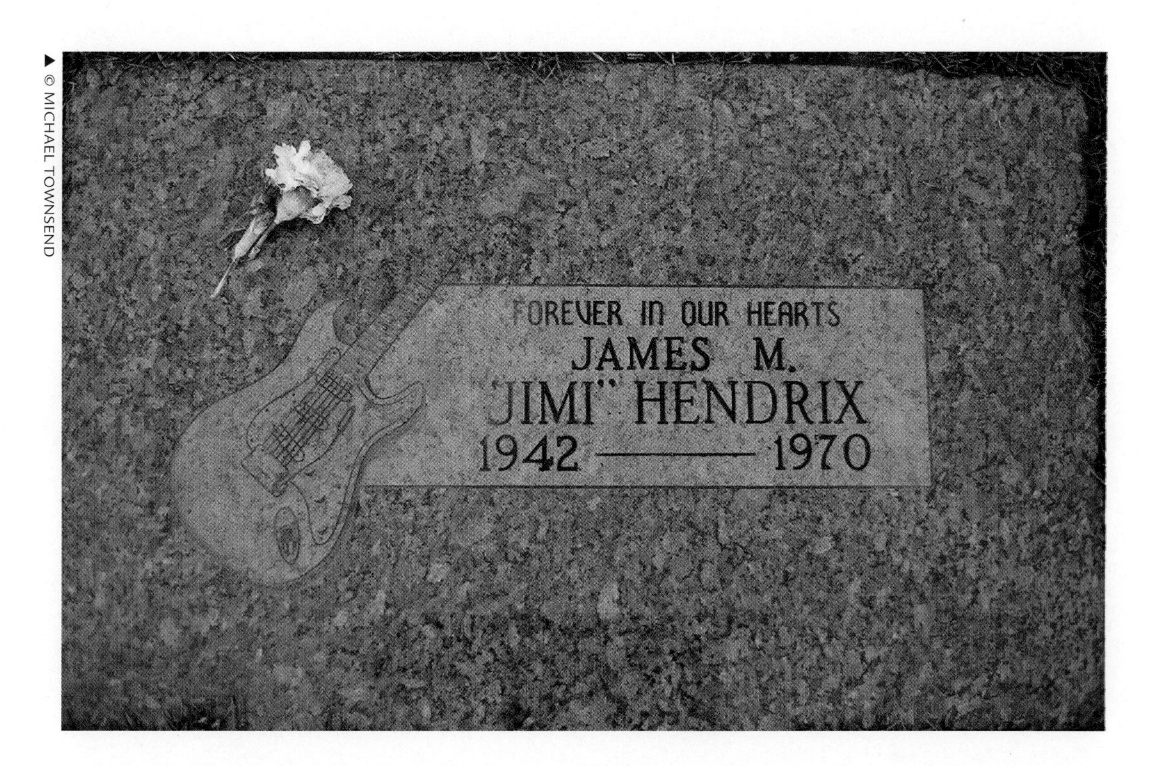

In many ways, modern Seattle still is like visiting that maiden aunt. The whites who make up three-quarters of the city's half-million population certainly don't all have those undemonstrative Scandinavian roots, but sometimes it seems that way. Newcomers do complain that the locals are polite enough, but they'll never invite you over for that barbecue.

African-Americans make up 10 percent of the population, Asians 11 percent, and Hispanics about 4 percent. That Scandinavian reservedness even seeps into those cultures. I've seen, for example, Mexican celebrations in Mexico. In Seattle, the Mexican-American weekend festival get-togethers are much more muted affairs. That's the Seattle style.

Other cities might have volatile city council meetings, for example, or public forums that turn into shouting matches. Here, we write a strongly worded letter to the editor after some careful research of the subject. The Seattle Public Library, after all, has the largest percentage of library cardholders of any other U.S. city—105 percent. OK, maybe that's fudging it a little bit, as that percentage includes county residents who don't live in the city limits.

The city's inherent politeness is a big reason why Seattle was so surprised at the melee of the 1999 protests when the World Trade Organization met here. Embarrassed by the magazine cover stories and evening news coverage of cops, tear gas, and confrontations, residents expressed much civic consternation about how Seattle had lost its innocence. In reality, the vandalism to downtown stores and buildings was committed by a few dozen out-of-town anarchist types. We never expected such impolite guests.

In typical Seattle fashion, within a few days, the streets were cleaned up and you couldn't tell any protests had taken place. This was the town that three days after the Great Fire of 1889—which started in a paint store and burned 60 city blocks—completely rebuilt its downtown commercial section. ▶

© BARRY WONG / SEATTLE TIMES

I like to believe that our politeness—and it is still very much here, despite the fact that our freeways are among the top-five most congested in the country, and despite the assorted problems that are part of any big city—is a major factor in placing Seattle on the world stage. We give room to people to just . . . try things.

It was the Pacific Northwest, away from Hollywood and its hype, that spawned the grunge music movement that became a worldwide phenomenon. It is here that Starbucks began its worldwide domination of coffeehouses. It is here that Craig McCaw, the cellular phone magnate, has his headquarters. It is here that Gary Larson, who had been working for the Seattle Humane Society, began drawing the first prototypes of what would become one of the most popular cartoon series in history—*The Far Side*. These people, although they can travel to sunnier locations, always come home. One reason is that Seattle is the kind of town that leaves its celebrities alone.

Allen can drop by a video store or go to a movie theater without fanfare. For many years, Larson was in a weekly pickup basketball game that I was part of; he finally, ruefully gave up hoops because of knee problems. During all that time, however, Larson simply was just another guy who loved the game, contributed his $2 to pay for the gym rental, and sometimes went out afterwards with the guys for some hamburgers. ▶

▲ © SEATTLE TIMES

▶ © HARLEY SOLTES / SEATTLE TIMES

John R. Grizz Deal—president and chief executive officer of Lizard Tech, a high-tech firm in our historic Pioneer Square—explains this phenomenon well. Mind you, there are now something like 2,200 software development firms in the area, plus 115 biotechnology firms. Many of them are headquartered in the downtown locations where the first pioneers started their lumber and trading businesses, doing their pioneering in the digital age.

Deal is in his late 30s—about the same age as many of the early entrepreneurs who founded this town. His office isn't far from where Henry Yesler's steam-powered sawmill allowed Seattle to first market timber that would be shipped to San Francisco and as far away as Australia. Marketing software that compresses data, Deal began LizardTech with $50, and expects to have revenues of $20 million next year.

Here's what Deal told me when he talked about why he moved his business here from Santa Fe: "I came here because the essence of Seattle is one of endless possibilities, not endless money. Seattle is where a couple of pretty smart kids met, and then, years later, returned to forge an entirely new part of the computer industry. Seattle is where, despite the rain, people can lead active outdoor lives, from water to mountains to desert within an hour or so. From Seattle, I can clearly see, and reach, Europe and Asia, enabling me to grow my business in three very different parts of the world.

"If I wax poetic, forgive me, but Seattle is everything I thought it would be when I moved here four years ago. People work hard in Seattle, from what I can see, because they want to contribute something to society as a whole, not just make money. Seattle is where you can enjoy living in a place big enough to have its own symphony, Paul Allen's Experience Music Project, a baseball team, a football team, museums, and rich history and culture, but it's small enough that you can actually be part of that culture."

I believe the early Seattle pioneers would nod approvingly at all these techies. They have become the town's new pioneers; their commerce now is digital instead of lumber. The techies have taken on with gusto the duties of civic boosterism. ▶

▶ © ELLEN M. BANNER / SEATTLE TIMES

The legacy of the old-time pioneers includes what is now the University of Washington campus, which boasts a world-renowned medical center. The campus was the site of the Alaska-Yukon-Pacific Exhibition of 1909. The Seattle Center, with its opera and Pacific Science Center, is the legacy of civic boosterism that created the 1962 World's Fair.

Now, it is high-tech money that literally has showered unprecedented millions of dollars onto Seattle. In 1999, Bill and Melinda Gates gave $30 million to United Way of King County. The McCaw family donated $20 million for a new performance hall at the Seattle Center. When the Seattle Seahawks football team was in trouble, Allen stepped up with $200 million to buy the franchise, and another $100 million to help build a new stadium. Allen's many other civic gifts include $1 million to the Children's Hospital and Medical Center, $15 million to the University of Washington, and $10 million to environmental groups.

A lifelong rock-and-roll fan, Allen splurged $240 million on building the interactive Experience Music Project, a tribute to his passion for the music. Onstage on opening day, he seemed like a kid at a birthday party.

Lesser-known techies also give plenty, and there is a booming local business in consultants who evaluate grant applications.

When I travel to other parts of the country, nobody ever asks me anymore if we get all the network channels. They ask me if I've ever spotted Gates in person; they ask me if Seattle really is such a number one place; they ask me if it really rains that much; and sometimes they ask me if I've caught a salmon.

Yes (at least I think that was Bill at the airport, no entourage around him), yes, yes, and yes.

As I finish writing this, the weather forecast calls for that rare sunshine in the next few days. I called a fishing charter captain; he was on his boat in Puget Sound and answered on his cell phone. Sure, he told me, we can go out and reel in a salmon.

You bet that when I go out, in the middle of Elliott Bay, I'll once again pause to savor the magnificent moment. Right now, right here, this is Seattle's time. ●

BELL STR

D I R E

EET PIER

T O R Y

ROUSTABOUT
SEATTLE, WA.

© TERRY DONNELLY

© MIKE SIEGEL/ SEATTLE TIMES

Color both natural and man-made suffuses Seattle's environs—especially around scenic Lake Union (OPPOSITE), where rainbow-resulting showers frequently soak the surrounds.

▼ © TERRY DONNELLY

Mount Rainier National Park (ABOVE) showcases the alpine vistas and pristine landscapes surrounding its namesake peak, the highest point in Washington State. On the other side of Puget Sound lies rocky Ruby Beach (OPPOSITE) in Olympic National Park. Dotted with a forest of driftwood, the beach is renowned for its majestic sea stacks—remnants of coastal walls that now stand alone in the water.

▲ © JIM CORWIN

One need not leave the city to see nature at its grandest. Given Seattle's superior quality of light, sunrise and sunset are often the most luminous times of day.

REDLINE

For the spirited residents of Seattle, every moment is like a walk in the woods. For John Gorman (BOTTOM), it's just another day at the office. Gorman is a forester with regionally based Simpson Timber.

▲ © DEAN RUTZ / SEATTLE TIMES

Bracketed by mountain ranges, the city offers many opportunities for its residents to scale new heights. And, although it's not the real thing, the 65-foot REI Pinnacle (OPPOSITE)—the world's tallest indoor climbing structure—attracts climbers from around the globe.

The oldest competitive swimmer in the Northwest, Jim Penfield (ABOVE) set a world record in his age group at the 2000 Seattle Masters. But not every Seattleite treats swimming as a contest: Many dive right in for recreation at places like Lake Silver (OPPOSITE TOP), or don scuba gear for a dip in Puget Sound (OPPOSITE BOTTOM).

© TOM REESE / SEATTLE TIMES

Butterflies flutter freely at the Woodland Park Zoo's exhibit *Butterflies and Blooms*, where visitors don't seem to mind serving as landing strips (RIGHT). Showing no fear, entomologist Don Ehlen comes face to face with his subjects—to the delight of the students who attend his Insect Safari presentations. Ehlen's passion has resulted in one of the world's largest private collections of insects.

Seattle reclaimed the land when it turned a decommissioned industrial site, originally used for converting coal to gas, into a public park. With a breathtaking view of Lake Union and the skyline, Gas Works Park features reliefs (OPPOSITE) designed by regional landscape architect Richard Haag. Some locals believe the city should now turn its improvement efforts toward urban eyesores such as the Alaskan Way Viaduct (PAGES 40 AND 41), described lovingly by a local newspaper columnist as "a thread between the cityscape and the Sound."

O.K. HOTEL
CAFE
LIVE ARTS · ENTERTAINMENT

DO NOT
DO NOT
ENTER

RAGE

Seattle offers its residents a unique window onto the world, with room enough for any emotion.

© KEVIN MCGOWAN / STRODE-MCGOWAN PHOTOGRAPHY

The Eiffel Tower is to Paris what the Space Needle is to Seattle. The landmark building, constructed for the 1962 World's Fair, casts a long shadow over the city.

EXIT 166
Stewart St.
Denny Way
1/2 MILE
EXIT 167
Mercer St
Fairview Ave
EXIT ONLY
Pike St.
RESTRICTED
City Center
Stewart St.
Howell St.
ONLY

Whatever the occasion, Seattle residents generally have a grand time participating. From the neighborhood Torchlight Parades of the annual Seafair to the Summer Solstice Festival, the city knows how to throw a party.

© JOHN & LISA MERRILL / DELIMONT, HERBIG & ASSOCIATES

© JOHN & LISA MERRILL / DELIMONT, HERBIG & ASSOCIATES

In addition to its many Seafair parades (TOP), Seattle also hosts the annual Antique and Classic Boat Show (MIDDLE) on Lake Washington and the Parade of Boats (OPPOSITE) along Montlake Cut. To watch less seaworthy vessels in action, boating fans attend the Seafair Milk Carton Derby (BOTTOM), featuring homemade, human-powered boats racing across Green Lake.

As the most northern port before Canada and the most western port before the Pacific Ocean, Seattle has seen a lot of activity—both military and commercial—in its waters since it was established. Several navy vessels, including the USS *Carl Vinson* (PAGES 52 AND 53), docked in Elliott Bay and offered free tours during Seafair in 1999.

HISTORICAL POINT OF INTEREST
THE U.S. NAVY'S "GREAT WHITE FLEET" ARRIVED
SEATTLE MAY 23 AND DEPARTED MAY 27, 1908 TO
CONTINUE THEIR FAMOUS 46,000 MILE ROUND THE
WORLD CRUISE. PART OF THE FLEET ANCHORED IN
ELLIOTT BAY NEAR THIS SITE AND THE CREWS
DISEMBARKED HERE AT THE FOOT OF LENORA AND
VIRGINIA STREETS - THEN KNOWN AS PIERS 9 & 10.
ERECTED NATIONAL MARITIME DAY 1961
PRESENTED BY
YUKON CLUB & PROPELLER CLUB - PORT OF SEATTLE

© RAY MEUSE

7

© BETTY UDESEN / SEATTLE TIMES

Patriotism sparkles in Seattle, where group reenactments of the Battle of Concorde join forces with more individual forms of self-expression to honor freedom. Many of those who lost their lives fighting for their country are entombed in the Evergreen-Washelli Cemetery (PAGES 56 AND 57) and remembered at the Washington State Memorial Wall (PAGES 58 AND 59).

CLANCY G
DRAKE
WASHINGTON
CAPTAIN
US MARINE CORPS
VIETNAM
DECEMBER 2 1931
DECEMBER 9 1965
PH & GS
CON W
REED
ARIZONA
WORLD WAR II
MAY 17 1910
WILLIAM
BERNARD
GARRISON
WASHINGTON
COMMANDER
US NAVY RET
WORLD WAR II
JAMES F
NAPIER
WASHINGTON
PVT
CECIL
ANDREW
PERRY
THOMPSON
WASHINGTON
DONALD
ARTHUR
KUKKONEN
WASHINGTON
JOHN W
LONG
RICHARD
HARRY
JOSEPH A
KEOHOOKALANI

1966
DUANE C SCHELL
LOUIE G FRITTS
LAWRENCE A FRANKLIN
THOMAS P MILLER
THOMAS P ROWLAND
JOHN E HIGMAN
PAUL H EKLUND
EVERETT B THOMPSON
DANNY A NETH
ALAN M TANGUAY
MARK J GARDELLA
BRUCE B LANDIS JR
CLYDE E MURR
PATRICK M DOYLE
ELWIN C WISE
WILLIAM R WEST
MARK S BLACK
SHAW SABINE IV
DALE L COURCHANE
DAVID M DAVIES
DONOVAN J PRUETT
STEVEN M SMITH
WATSON WILLIS

▲ © JIM CORWIN

Call it the Pacifist Northwest: Antiviolence protestors make their causes known through a variety of body languages. Considered by many to be the grandfather of the local movement, Dr. Floyd Schmoe (OPPOSITE) has worked in Hiroshima, Korea, and the Middle East to rebuild homes and reopen wells destroyed by war. During the 1990s, he was nominated for the Nobel Peace Prize four years in a row.

The locally grown Boeing Company draws hundreds of spectators to day-long ceremonies that herald the launching of each new model. The company has been a major presence in the area since 1916.

BOEING 7
ILFC
JAS
saudia
malaysia

Dressed for success: He may be a local, but Microsoft cofounder Bill Gates (LEFT) is a player on the global stage. The computer guru, who has long held claim to being one of the world's richest men, helped start a technological revolution when his company opened its doors in 1975. At the helm of another of the city's innovative corporations, Boeing Chairman and CEO Phil Condit (OPPOSITE) has been an aviation enthusiast all his life, earning his pilot's license at age 18 and working at Boeing for more than 30 years.

When it comes to good books, everybody in Seattle is on the same page. David Guterson (OPPOSITE) won the prestigious PEN/Faulkner Award in 1995 for his first novel, *Snow Falling on Cedars*, set in the Pacific Northwest during the 1940s. That same year, Jeff Bezos (BOTTOM) launched Amazon.com, which has grown to become one of the largest retailers on the Internet, shipping goods across the globe.

Elegance is always in fashion in Seattle, whether in the beguiling curves of a dress (RIGHT) by local designer Susan St. Clair, or in a concerto conducted by Seattle Symphony Orchestra music director Gerard Schwarz (OPPOSITE).

Seattle has a reputation for public performances both musical and dramatic. For the 100th episode of *Frasier*, the cast and crew of the popular sitcom—including Kelsey Grammer (OPPOSITE, STANDING) and David Hyde Pierce (OPPOSITE, KNEELING)—filmed on the streets of Seattle, accompanied by the many musicians who give free virtuoso performances each day.

Undeterred by the constant threat of wedding-day showers, Seattle couples celebrate their nuptials in grand style.

▲ © JIM CORWIN

Not only in Seattle but throughout its environs, people gather for events featuring lots of food and lots of music. At the annual Ballard Seafood Fest (ABOVE), an Elvis impersonator puts the King in King County, while reggae musicians bring Caribbean rhythms to the Kent Canterbury Faire (OPPOSITE).

As the calendar cycles through, Seattleites find many opportunities to go round and round. Each winter, the Christmas Carousel in Westlake Square (OPPOSITE) takes holiday revelers for a spin.

Held each Memorial Day weekend, the annual Folklife Fest (OPPOSITE) gives attendees many golden opportunities to see the world's ethnic, folk, and traditional arts in full bloom. For more fun, locals can go carouseling on Pier 57's ornate merry-go-round (BOTTOM) or carousing at Goldie's tavern (TOP) in the Wallingford District.

From scrap metal, area artist Dan Klennert (LEFT) creates larger-than-life sculptures as part of his playful *Recycled Spirits of Iron* outdoor collection, located near Elbe. During the hot summers, children frolic in the Seattle Center's oversized International Fountain (OPPOSITE BOTTOM), which many regard as charmingly ugly.

SAFECO FIELD
LEFT FIELD

Out along Highway 99 lie the remains of what must have been one giant cowboy. The concrete Hat 'N Boots (ABOVE) was erected during the 1950s as part of a filling station, and has survived weather and vandalism to become a local monument to kitsch. To catch sight of a giant baseball mitt—as well as a big game—fans can head toward Safeco Field (OPPOSITE), the new home of the Seattle Mariners.

▲ © SEATTLE TIMES

▲ © JIM BATES

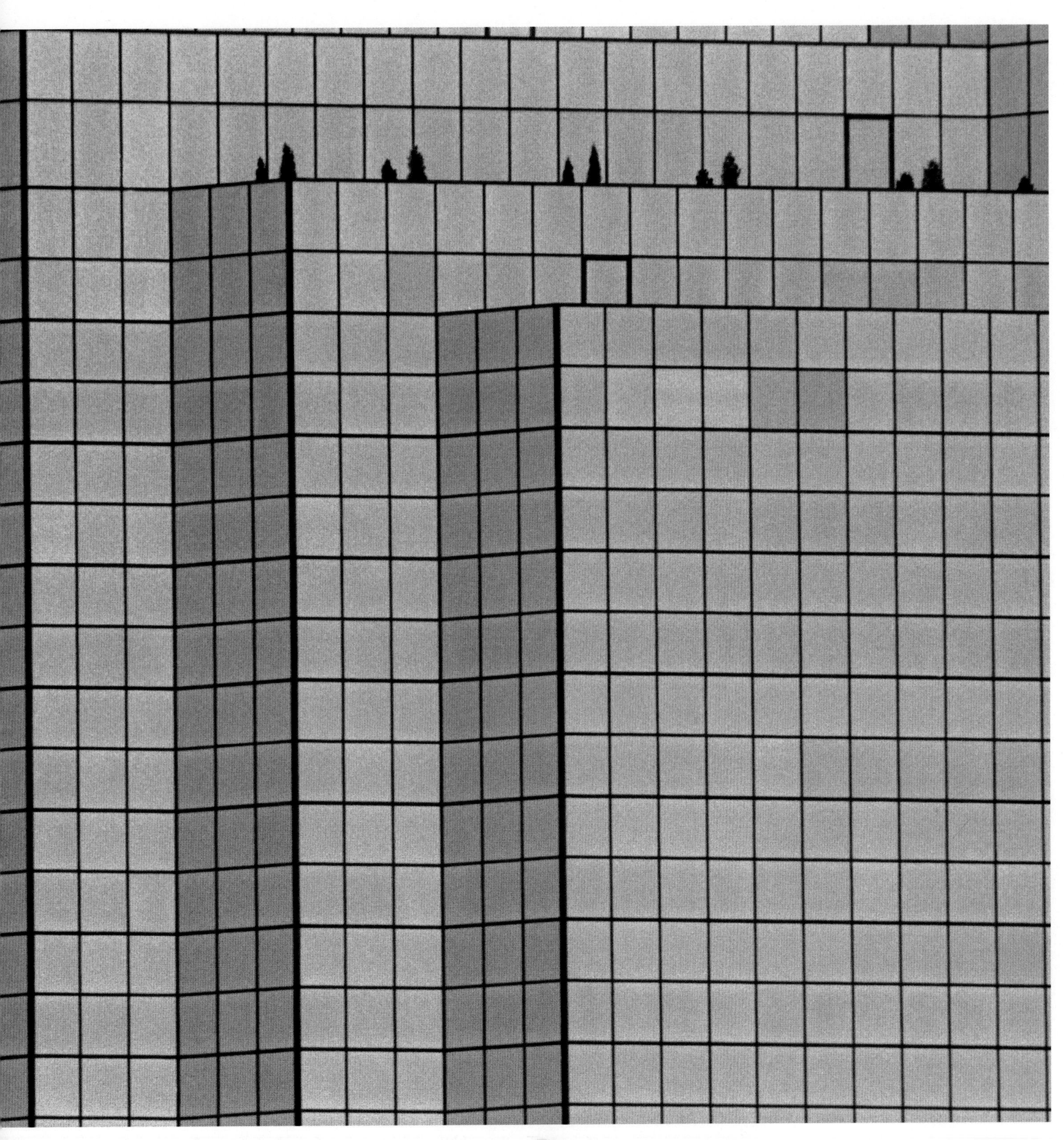

During the 1800s, impossibly tall trees like the mighty Douglas Fir (OPPOSITE) brought loggers and pioneers to the Northwest in droves. Today, the lumber industry is still branching out, but even the tallest forests are dwarfed by Seattle's modern skyscrapers.

CHUCK
OSE
FEBRUARY 18
~ MAY 9, 1999
SEATTL

Designed by local architect Robert Venturi and opened in 1991, the Seattle Art Museum (LEFT) houses more than 23,000 works of art in its quiet, spacious galleries. By contrast, Joseph Borofsky's 11-ton, motorized *Hammering Man* sculpture (OPPOSITE) pounds a constant rhythm near the museum's entrance.

Public art and sculpture flourish throughout Seattle, often incorporating the office buildings and popular landmarks that surround them. Designed by Alexander Liberman and erected in 1984, the gigantic, 45-foot *Olympic Iliad* (LEFT) greets visitors at the Broad Street entrance to the Seattle Center.

© RAY MEUSE

NOW

© JIM CORWIN

▲ © JIM CORWIN

The legendary Kingdome and the new Safeco Field once were across the street neighbors—but no longer. Opened in 1976, the Kingdome—the world's largest concrete dome—was demolished on March 26, 2000, one day before its 24th anniversary. Using nearly 4,500 pounds of dynamite, the city flattened 25,000 tons of concrete in just 16.8 seconds (PAGES 90 THROUGH 93).

BYE
BYE
KINGDOME!

Immediately following the blasts that crumbled the Kingdome came an unusual memorial to the structure many saw as a cultural landmark and others viewed as an eyesore. A cloud some 500 feet high cloaked the surrounding area, blanketing buildings, cars, and people with a thick film of dust.

Whether at work or at play, Seattleites have never been shy about getting their hands dirty—or their faces, for that matter—to do the job right.

Serious and novice marathoners make tracks in a number of events like the popular St. Patrick's Day Mad Dash (RIGHT) or the Bothell Fun Run (OPPOSITE BOTTOM). Less competitive runners can take a leisurely jog along the Seattle Waterfront, where bronze statues keep the pace (OPPOSITE TOP).

A constant presence at the top of the American League West, the Seattle Mariners (LEFT) played their first outdoor game when they moved from the Kingdome to the open-air Safeco Field in 1999. The Seattle Seahawks (OPPOSITE) have experienced their own ups and downs since starting play on August 1, 1976, but have always enjoyed the undying loyalty of thousands of devoted fans.

SPALDING
NBA
GRANT
54
SPURS

Hoops enthusiasts get a double shot of their favorite sport with the WNBA Seattle Storm (LEFT), which finished its inaugural season in 2000, and the NBA SuperSonics (OPPOSITE), consistently ranked among the top teams in the Pacific Division.

A favorite among competitive swimmers as well as those making a splash just for fun, the King County Aquatic Center (OPPOSITE) hosts a number of national events, including the 1999 U.S. Synchronized Swimming Team Trials.

Alamo

In Seattle, some children begin participating in sports at a very early age, either through organized teams or through less structured games at backyard birthday parties.

In Seattle, cultures and creeds are displayed with regal fervor and unmatched pride. Parades and festivities throughout the region give locals many opportunities to share their heritage.

SFD
SFD

Residents commemorate the 1889 Great Seattle Fire, which destroyed more than 50 city blocks, with the annual Fire Festival. In 1998, the city unveiled the Seattle Fallen Firefighters Memorial (OPPOSITE), designed by local artist Hai Ying Wu and composed of four bronze figures at Pioneer Square in Occidental Park.

◆ © DANIEL KIM / SEATTLE TIMES

Onlookers might mistake the homes on East John Street (OPPOSITE) for lean-tos, but they are in fact high-demand housing. Other residences stand straight and tall, as distinctive as the individuals who own them.

PIONEER BUILDING
ZASU
PIONEER BUILDING
PIONEER SQU

At the turn of the century, gold rushers en route to Alaska stayed at the State Hotel, now known as the Delmar Building (LEFT). Named after such lodgers, the Pioneer Building (OPPOSITE), constructed in 1892, was designed by architect Elmer Fisher in the Romanesque Revival style, featuring pronounced Roman arches around its windows.

With an overarching sense of scale, Seattle's urban landscape frames its day-to-day activities. Whether at work or at play, residents of all ages mingle with both the natural and the man-made elements of the city (PAGES 116-119).

STOP
TOYOTA

There's more than one way to reach the top. Outdoorsmen at the Marymoor Park in nearby Redmond (LEFT) depend on rock-climbing tools to aid their ascent. But for students at the University of Washington—under the watchful gaze of the cast-stone figures adorning Suzzallo Library (OPPOSITE)—it's brains, not brawn, that lead to success.

The waters around Seattle spawn all kinds of fun. Salmon swimming upstream through the Hiram M. Chittendon locks in Ballard are close enough to touch as they navigate their way through a fish ladder that gradually acclimates them back into a saltwater environment. Area kayakers adopt a more adventurous approach, immersing themselves full force in their activities.

CHARLIE'S PRODUCE
05

FARMERS MARKET
DOWN UNDER

Farmers from throughout the Pacific Northwest sell some of the region's finest foods at the famous Pike Place Market, the oldest continuously operating farmers market in the United States. A favorite spot among tourists and locals alike, the market features scores of booths displaying schools of fresh fish, as well as colorful fruits, vegetables, and flowers—all in a lively atmosphere.

Mercer Island
NEXT 2 EXITS
SPEED LIMIT 60
EXIT 6
W Mercer Wy
1½ MILES
SPEED LIMIT 60

Whether on the outskirts or through the heart of the city, transporting traffic over Seattle's lakes requires some fancy bridgework. Floating bridges and more traditional structures reflect a city on the move.

ELEPHANT
Super
CAR WASH

RECYCLED

Making vehicles sparkle might be the job of the local car wash, but Goldfield, Nevada, folk artist Slim Sirnes found a different way to put a shine on his wheels. An entrant in the Seattle Art Car Blow-Out 2000, Sirnes truck *Recycled* is adorned with thousand of bottle caps and aluminum cans that shine night or day.

Seattle's volatile relationship with the many vehicles that traverse its highways can be traced back to Ralph S. Hopkins' three-horsepower Woods Electric (OPPOSITE), the city's first horseless carriage. Traffic congestion inspires not only public transportation, but public art as well: At least one car has met an unsavory fate in the giant hands of the Fremont Troll (PAGES 132 AND 133), which hides out under the Aurora Avenue Bridge.

Situated since 1895 in the aptly named University District, the University of Washington-Seattle teaches its students to view the world from their own unique perspectives.

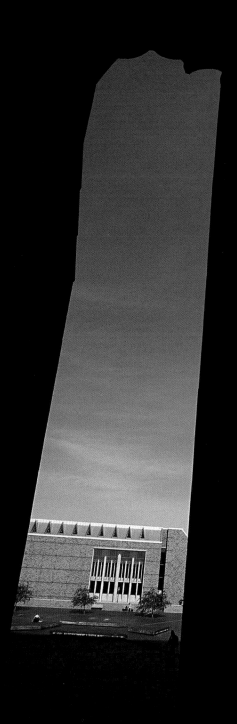

Originally envisioned by Henry Suzzallo—University of Washington's 15th president—as "the soul of the university," the Suzzallo Library was completed in 1926 and stands today as a monument to knowledge and learning among the Gothic buildings on campus.

SALOMON

Whether crowd-surfing in the mosh pit or skateboarding on the half pipe, Seattle's youths throw themselves into everything they do.

While he didn't set his guitar on fire like his hero did at the Monterey Pop Festival, Jimi Hendrix fan—and Microsoft cofounder—Paul Allen (RIGHT) did smash a glass version of the instrument at the opening of his Experience Music Project museum in June 2000. Attracting thousands of music lovers from across the country, the inaugural event featured concerts by rock legends like Bo Diddley (OPPOSITE TOP) and newcomers like Beck.

Designed by world-renowned architect Frank Gehry, the Experience Music Project's curvaceous, psychedelic exterior reflects its whimsical interior and numerous installations. The museum—with some 80,000 rock, blues, soul, jazz, country, and rap artifacts—emphasizes interactive exhibits that allow visitors to play rare instruments in the Sound Lab and peruse an exhaustive virtual library.

© JIM BATES

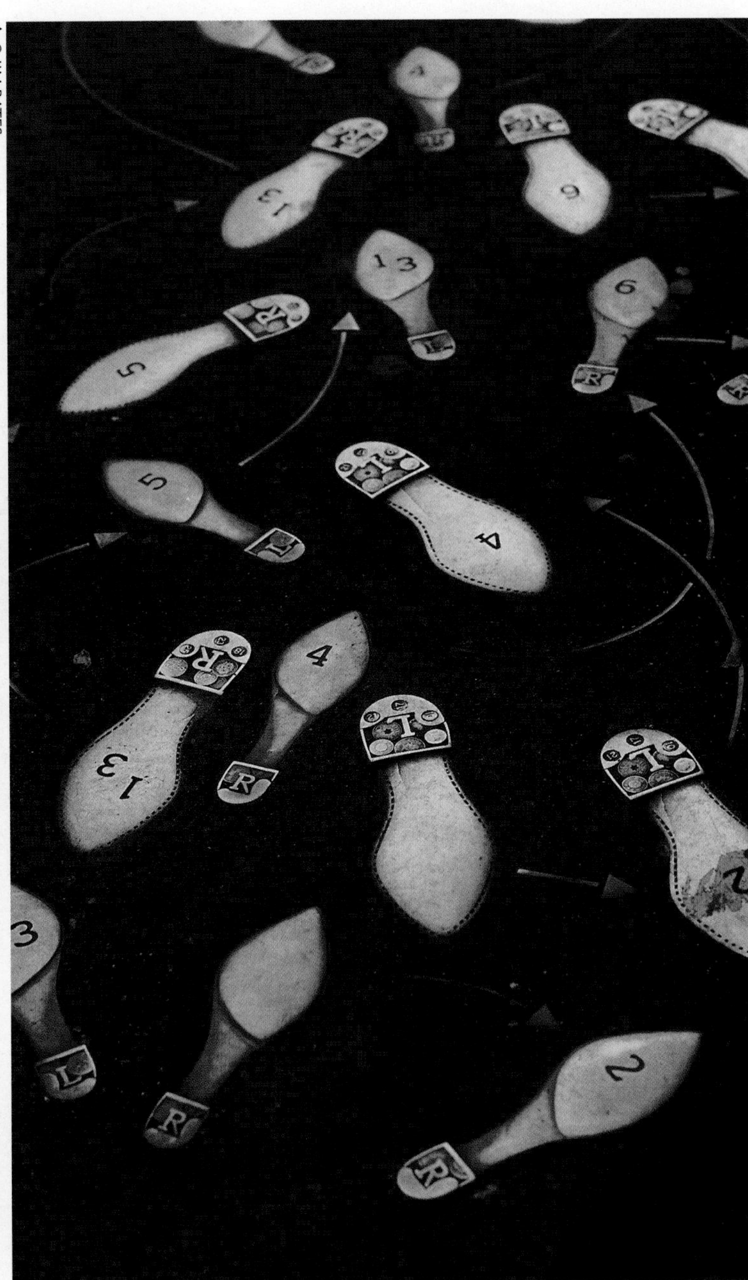

While some Seattleites live life on the edge, others simply dance there. Members of Montreal-based Cirque du Soleil (LEFT) perform their nimble dance moves on the Space Needle's halo—520 feet above the ground. And in the don't-try-this-at-home category, members of the Project Bandaloop troupe (OPPOSITE) execute aerial moves on the side of the structure.

During summer's hottest days, Seattleites don swimwear and head to water parks and pools to cool off. But at winter's icy peak, they don snow gear and make the pilgrimage to places like Snoqualmie Falls (LEFT) to view nature in all its gelid grandeur.

Winter finds the Pacific Northwest in full frozen bloom, its natural and rustic charm enhanced by a menagerie of icicles and a dusting of snow.

© THOMAS JAMES HURST / SEATTLE TIMES

Each year, hundreds gather beneath Seattle's Bon Marche star for the annual lighting of the Christmas tree in Westlake Center (OPPOSITE). Testing the limits of the city's generosity, crowds of a different sort turned out to demonstrate against the World Trade Organization, which met in the city in 1999. At several points, riot police were called in to quell violence.

▼ © ALAN BERNER / SEATTLE TIMES

▲ © JIMI LOTT / SEATTLE TIMES

Illumination and celebration go hand in hand in Seattle. To ring in the new millennium, thousands of residents of all ages gathered at the Seattle Center for the Reflecting Fire ceremony (RIGHT). And each year, the city's Jewish community sponsors a large menorah at Westlake Park in observance of Hanukkah.

During Seattle's Chinese New Year parade, traditional lion dances ward off bad spirits and give participants an opportunity to really get into the celebration. Elements of a vital Asian presence appear throughout the city, where some 11 percent of the population descends from the Far East.

Seattle's fascination with outer space has resulted in some truly far-out landmarks. Erected in 1994, the Fremont Rocket (LEFT)—an authentic 1950s rocket overlooking the corner of Evanston Avenue and North 35th Street—stands ready for blast-off. The city's most recognizable skyline feature, the Space Needle (OPPOSITE), glows like a flying saucer when the stars come out, but the courtyard of the nearby Pacific Science Center (PAGES 160 AND 161), designed for the 1962 World's Fair by local architect Minoru Yamasaki, recalls Venice more than Venus.

Whether enjoying a romantic sunset at Green Lake (BOTTOM) or studying trees at the Washington Park Arboretum (OPPOSITE BOTTOM), Seattle residents have plenty of places to enjoy the fiery colors that saturate the city each fall.

The Pacific Northwest is home to a vast population of wild animals, but in such an idyllic setting, the wildest of wildlife might just be the locals (PAGES 164-167).

Located about an hour north of Seattle, Skagit Valley inspires intense tulipomania. Each year, the area attracts some 800,000 enthusiasts looking to tiptoe through its colorful fields.

While Seattle's highways are packed with fast-paced vehicles, its sidewalks and walkways host the easygoing foot traffic of the many people out to just enjoy the view.

UNIVERSITY
SEA FOOD
POULTRY
Fresh

Although they won't taste very good poached or grilled, the fish sold at the weekly Fremont Sunday Market (LEFT) make for eye-catching decorations. But for seafood that is both fresh and edible, Seattle offers any number of fine fisheries and eateries to sate the appetite.

Ordered and organized objects around Seattle reveal the city's on-going activity and development—from road construction to heavy industry—as well as all the fun to be had.

Each day, some 75,000 passengers on some 1,300 flights travel through Seattle-Tacoma International Airport—or, as it is popularly known, Sea-Tac. With such figures growing steadily, the airport is undergoing a massive improvement and expansion plan—adding a new runway and enlarging its terminals—to be completed in 2010.

Birds of a completely different feather sometimes do flock together. More often, however, the opposite is true, as the many formations of Canadian geese flying over the area certainly prove.

◀ © KEVIN MCGOWAN / STRODE-MCGOWAN PHOTOGRAPHY

The Museum of Flight in Seattle ignites the fancy of children and adults alike. The glass-and-steel Great Gallery (RIGHT) features a squadron's worth of authentic planes, including a gigantic B-47 suspended from the ceiling, as well as precise replicas of such historic flyers as the Wright brothers' first plane. The Red Barn (ABOVE), a replica of Boeing's original building, houses smaller exhibits on everything from aviation history to space travel.

FLIGHT TAKES OFF
FLIGHT TAKES OFF
TRANSPORTS
TRANSPORTS
U.S. AIR MAIL
NC10655

▼ © LEE FOSTER

Considering Dr. Martin Luther King Jr. a true hero, Washington residents commemorate his legacy in a number of ways. In particular, Seattle honors his memory with Martin Luther King Jr. Park (OPPOSITE), which centers around a 30-foot granite sculpture created by the late artist Robert Kelly.

STOP THE
BOMBING!
mazda

In the shadow of Mount Rainier, the city remains a center for culture and the arts, and has earned its status as the world's technological and commercial capital. With even greater successes on the horizon, Seattle's time has truly come.

Profiles in Excellence

A look at the corporations, businesses, professional groups, and community service organizations that have made this book possible. Their stories-offering an informal chronicle of the local business community-are arranged according to the date they were established in Seattle.

The Ackerley Group
Activate Corporation
Airborne Express
AT&T Wireless Services
Attachmate Corporation
The Benaroya Company
The Boeing Company
Boullioun Aviation Services, Inc.
The Burnsteads
Children's Hospital and Regional Medical Center
Christian Faith Center
The City Church
City University
Costco Wholesale
Covenant Celebration Church
Dilettante Chocolates
Expedia, Inc.
The 5th Avenue Theatre
Fran's Chocolates
Freddie's Club Casino
Gene Juarez Salons & Spas
Insignia International Inc.
John F. Buchan Homes
NikeTown

verlake Christian Church
acific Science Center
acifiCare of Washington
innacle Realty Management Company
uality Business Systems
ealNetworks, Inc.
abey Corporation
andusky Radio
eattle Homes and Lifestyles
eattle Pacific University
eattle Public Utilities
eattle Theatre Group

Starbucks
Torero's Mexican Restaurants
United Airlines
Virginia Mason Medical Center
W Hotel
Wade Cook Financial Corporation
Washington CEO Magazine
Western Wireless Corporation/
VoiceStream Wireless Corporation
Wizards of the Coast

1891–1969

1891	Seattle Pacific University
1895	Seattle Public Utilities
1907	Children's Hospital and Regional Medical Center
1916	The Boeing Company
1920	Virginia Mason Medical Center
1926	United Airlines
1926	The 5th Avenue Theatre
1946	Airborne Express
1956	The Benaroya Company
1957	The Burnsteads
1961	John F. Buchan Homes
1962	Pacific Science Center
1968	Overlake Christian Church

SINCE ITS BEGINNINGS MORE THAN A CEN TURY AGO, SEATTLE PACIFIC UNIVERSITY (SPU) HAS BUILT A SOLID REPUTATION ON TH COMPETENCE AND CHARACTER OF ITS GRADUATES, THE QUALITY OF ITS ACADEMI PROGRAMS, AND THE IMPACT OF ITS SERVICE IN THE COMMUNITY. THIS THREE-PART COM MITMENT REFLECTS SPU'S MISSION AS A CHRISTIAN UNIVERSITY DEDICATED TO THE LIBERA ARTS, SCIENCES, AND PROFESSIONS. ● FOUNDED IN 1891 BY FREE METHODIS pioneers, SPU holds to a Christian tradition based on the idea that faith and intellect are not incompatible. More than 50 denominations are represented on the campus from a variety of faith traditions. The university's faith-based commitment links the growth of academic competence with the formation of personal character.

SPU's student body currently numbers some 3,400, with the majority of students coming from Washington, Oregon, and California. Overall, the university draws students from 36 states and 51 countries. SPU is consistently ranked among the western region's top-tier universities, and has been designated one of the region's top 10 Best College Values by *U.S. News & World Report.*

THE SEATTLE PACIFIC UNIVERSITY (SPU) CAMPUS, LOCATED ON 35 ACRES IN SEATTLE'S PICTURESQUE QUEEN ANNE NEIGHBORHOOD, COMBINES TURN-OF-THE-CENTURY ARCHITECTURE WITH MODERN BUILDINGS IN A PARKLIKE SETTING (RIGHT).

SPU OFFERS WHAT MANY REGIONAL COLLEGES AND UNIVERSITIES CANNOT: A BALANCE BETWEEN INTELLECTUAL GROWTH AND THE DEVELOPMENT OF FAITH (LEFT).

Agents of Change

For the new millennium, the university's motto is Engaging the Culture, Changing the World. This vision of SPU President Philip W. Eaton's is the force behind the university's comprehensive planning efforts.

Change will also come in the more tangible form of new buildings on campus, increased emphasis on science education, and new endowed chairs at the university. Plans to build a 63,000-square-foot science facility call for construction to begin in 2002. A chapel/concert hall that would accommodate 1,800 people and provide a state-of-the-art venue for the university's acclaimed choral and instrumental groups is also forthcoming.

"I believe the people of Seattle Pacific University are prepared in striking new ways to be powerful change agents in our community and in the world," Eaton says. "That's a bold claim for our university, and yet I believe it with all my heart."

Campus Life

The SPU campus, located on 35 acres in Seattle's picturesque Queen Anne neighborhood, combines turn-of-the-century architecture with modern buildings in a parklike setting. The university also operates a 965-acre wilderness campus on Blakely Island, as well as a 150-acre seaside campus on Whidbey Island.

More than 22 percent of the university's students are involved in graduate and postbaccalaureate studies, reflecting SPU's commitment to a comprehensive range of programs aimed at graduate and undergraduate students. The university offers 10 master's degree pro grams and two doctoral programs. Undergraduate instruction puts a premium on teaching and individual interaction; 75 percent of the under graduate classes have enrollments o 30 or fewer, and the overall student faculty ratio is 16-to-1.

Athletics are another aspect of SPU's identity. The school offers 35 men's, women's, and coed activi ties on the intramural side, as well as competitive intercollegiate programs in gymnastics, crew, soccer, track and field, cross country, and volleyball. The basketball program earned national attention in 2000, when the men's team reached the NCAA Final Four for Division II with an impressive regular season record of 27-5.

Seattle Pacific University offers what many regional colleges and uni versities cannot: a balance between intellectual growth and the develop ment of faith. As the list of alumni grows and flourishes, the university will continue to cultivate agents of change for the future.

With more than 70 years of service, nited Airlines is committed to being the premier airline in the world by mainaining a strong, recognizable corporate identity—incorporating the rousing easures of Gershwin's *Rhapsody in Blue* and the signature phrase Fly the Friendly kies—and by focusing intensely on developing and improving air travel for its illions of passengers. "Our mission," says Terry Brady, city manager of United irlines' Seattle operation, "is to be cognized worldwide as the airline f choice."

The company was founded in eattle in 1926, when airmail was an dventure as well as a convenience. he United name first appeared in 28, when the United Aircraft and ransport Corporation was formed a holding company for another eattle fixture, the Boeing Airplane ompany. United Airlines was offially organized in 1931.

Today, the company is the largest r carrier in the world, with flights 134 destinations in 27 countries and ne U.S. territory. The roster includes rgentina, Australia, Belgium, Brazil, anada, Chile, Costa Rica, El Salvaor, France, Germany, Guatemala, aly, Japan, Korea, Mexico, the Nethlands, New Zealand, the People's epublic of China, Peru, Puerto Rico, ingapore, Taiwan, Thailand, the nited Kingdom, Uruguay, and enezuela, not to mention locations roughout the United States. Overl, United offers more than 2,400 aily departures. The numbers quickly become mind-boggling: 550 aircraft, some 237,995 passengers per day, more than 100,000 employees worldwide, and almost 15 billion seat miles. The company generated $17.6 billion in total revenue in 1998, with fully distributed net earnings of $1.31 billion.

Roots in Seattle

Though United's headquarters is in Chicago, the company's roots are still in Seattle, which remains a significant component of the overall international system. Approximately 1,800 employees are based in the Emerald City, and United sends 50 flights out of Sea-Tac International Airport daily, part of an estimated 4 million Seattle passengers annually. The company is involved locally in various community organizations, and employees volunteer their time in numerous local projects, including United Way's Day of Caring. "Seattle really represents the bread and butter of our business: business travel," Brady says. "It's an integral part of our West Coast Gateway strategy."

A Reputation for Innovation

United has recently unveiled a number of new innovations, including Economy Plus, a $300 million aircraft improvements program designed to improve the experience of coach flight. Legroom, work space, and seat pitch have been increased to accommodate the needs of business travelers. On the first-class side, the airline has introduced suites with beds to soothe the weary. Seattle is a direct target for another new wrinkle: E-ticketing, which allows customers to purchase tickets on-line. To complement the service, United offers self-service machines for boarding passes, allowing passengers to skip the lines and hassles of airline gates. So far, Seattle is the largest user of E-ticketing services of any city where United has a presence.

"Seattle is one of our big targets for innovations," says Brady. With a strong identity and reputation for quality and innovation, United will be flying high for years to come.

Since 1926, United Airlines has grown to become the premier air carrier in the world—today with flights to 134 destinations in 27 countries and one U.S. territory.

The history of Seattle's water, soli waste, and engineering utilities spans the past century, and Seattle Publi Utilities (SPU) continues to serve the city's citizens and businesses in the ne millennium. Seattle has grown upward and outward on the roads, bridge watersheds, seawalls, sewers, and electrical systems built by SPU. l It wasn' easy in the early days. As a frontier outpost without reliable water o

a public sewage system, Seattle was severely challenged by its growing population to make the region safe for habitation. In 1889, two crises moved the city forward: a typhoid outbreak from sewage-polluted Lake Union and the Great Fire.

The spread of the deadly typhoid epidemic convinced the city council to listen to the health and water officials and build separate systems for sewage and water. City engineers began developing a protected water supply high in the Cascade Mountains, with a system of pipelines and reservoirs still owned and operated by the city today. The second crisis was the Great Fire that eliminated the 64-acre business district, leaving nothing standing. After the fire, Seattle was rebuilt in brick, arising from the ashes as a city of substance with the beginnings of the infrastructure it still uses today.

In the 21st century, new challenges face Seattle and the Puget Sound. To meet those challenges, SPU was formed in 1997, consolidating the Water and Engineering departments to include Engineering Services, the Solid Waste Utility, and the Drainage and Wastewater Utility. This consolidation gives Seattle residents one-stop shopping for all water, sewage, flood control, garbage, and recycling utility services.

The watersheds used by Seattle Public Utilities (SPU) gather and store rain and snowmelt for more than 1.3 million people in the greater Seattle area. More than 160 million gallons of clean, reliable, and inexpensive water is delivered daily from the protected boundaries of the Tolt River and Cedar River watersheds.

SPU provides a new, stronger focus on seamless customer service, environmental stewardship, and inte grated utility operations. By forgin partnerships with Seattle residents, with schools and businesses, and through educational programs, goa are being met in the neighborhood and business districts.

SPU is restoring portions of Seattle's four largest creeks through the Urban Creeks Legacy Program. While restoring habitat for salmon and other wildlife is the primary goal of the effort, the works will also improve drainage, prevent erosion and flooding, and improve community open spaces and trails. Volunteer creek stewards pick up trash, plant trees, remove weeds, build trails, and have fun.

An Environmental Steward

SPU sponsors numerous program throughout Seattle to address environmental concerns. Stewardshi Through Environmental Partnership (STEP) supports community-base water quality protection. Friends o Recycling, Adopt a Street, Master Composters, and other green program have brought citizen volunteers, businesspeople, and schoolchildren together with a common goal—to keep the community and its businesse healthy, and to protect Seattle's envi ronment for future generations. Seattle is a city of people who get involved, and in recognizing this spectacular asset, SPU continually seeks ways to strengthen communication with the residents and businesses it serves.

Because environmental preservation so essential, SPU is leading the way water conservation and restoring ·attle's urban creek habitats. In July 99, the city council approved SPU's odel Habitat Conservation Plan r the Cedar River Watershed. Also, e Urban Creeks Legacy Project helps store salmon habitat in the region a gift for future generations.

Other programs to increase salmon pulations on Washington's rivers ve reaped rewards, including the edar River Interim Sockeye Salmon atchery and projects on the Tolt ver, where summer steelhead are turning in growing numbers.

The new Tolt River Treatment Facility, Seattle's first water filtration plant, is expected to become operational in late 2000. This facility will be a 120 million-gallon-per-day filtration and ozonation plant for treatment of Seattle's Tolt River, which provides about a third of the water for Greater Seattle. Filtration will improve water quality to a level far beyond existing standards, and will also allow the reservoir to be operated in all weather conditions, producing an additional water supply from the Tolt Reservoir.

By using an innovative, public-private partnership for the development of the Tolt River project, the City of Seattle will save taxpayers an estimated $70 million over the cost of doing business the old way. With the use of a design-build-operate (DBO) model, rather than the conventional design-bid-procurement model, proposers are asked to develop their own concepts on how best to achieve performance specifications. This new procedure encourages teams to use their entrepreneurial initiative to provide the best solution, and makes one firm responsible, eliminating layers of suppliers and the associated costs.

Water, sewers and drainage, solid waste collection, and disposal, all in one place—SPU provides a seamless, single contact for utility services. The utility is focused on protection of Seattle's infrastructure so businesses can keep doing what they do best, while environmental stewardship and protection of the area's natural resources define its vision. Simply put, this is what Seattle Public Utilities is all about.

CLOCKWISE FROM TOP LEFT:
THE NEW TOLT TREATMENT FACILITY IS A 120-MILLION-GALLON-PER-DAY (MGD) FILTRATION AND OZONATION PLANT FOR TREATMENT OF SEATTLE'S TOLT RIVER WATER SUPPLY, WHICH PROVIDES ABOUT ONE-THIRD OF THE WATER FOR SEATTLE AND ITS 26 REGIONAL WHOLESALE CUSTOMERS.

SEATTLE IS COMMITTED TO BRINGING BACK HEALTHY SALMON RUNS. SPU AND OTHER CITY DEPARTMENTS WHOSE DAILY OPERATIONS CAN IMPACT THE ENVIRONMENT ARE WORKING HARD TO EASE THOSE EFFECTS TO MAKE THE ENVIRONMENT FRIENDLIER FOR FISH AND WILDLIFE.

SPU IS PARTNERING WITH COMMUNITY GROUPS TO ENSURE LONG-TERM STEWARDSHIP, AND IS EDUCATING SCHOOLCHILDREN AND ADULTS ABOUT COMMON ACTIVITIES THAT HAVE AN EFFECT ON SALMON.

Children's Hospital and Regional Medical Center

No one knows children like Children's is a phrase families of the Pacific Northwest can relate to from the deepest leve of experience. Since 1907, Children's Hospital and Regional Medical Center ha been a wellspring of emotional support for its young patients and their familie and has grown to become a medical and research facility of national stature. From the tragic loss of a child rose a vision of pediatric care that woul transform thousands of lives: Anna Clise, a prominent woman in turn-of-the-century Seattle, acted on her vision by pledging her life and resources to build a hospital for children. Thanks to her tender concern and dedicated efforts, a group of 23 friends at the Seattle Chamber of Commerce pledged $20 each to get the project off the ground. Their support and resources laid the foundation for Children's Hospital and Regional Medical Center.

Though Children's has changed dramatically since 1907, the organization remains true to Clise's mission—to care for all children of the Pacific Northwest. Today, Children's is a state-of-the-art pediatric referral center, with 40 outpatient clinics, 2,500 employees, and a network of critical care ground and air transport that brings patients from community hospitals throughout Washington, Alaska, Montana, and Idaho. "We draw patients from probably the largest land mass in the country as a children's hospital," says Treuman Katz, president and chief executive officer.

Children's Hospital and Regional Medical Center provides the highest-quality medical care, combining the latest medical research with compassion and understanding for the special needs of children and their families (left).

Since 1907, Children's Hospital has been a wellspring of emotional support for its young patients and their families, and has grown to become a medical and research facility of national stature (right).

ALAN CRAFT

Excellence in Care, Education, and Research

Children's provides the highest-quality medical care, combining the latest medical research with compassion and understanding for the special needs of children and their families. Children's is the pediatric teaching hospital for the University of Washington School of Medicine, with the Department of Pediatrics based at Children's. The hospital also maintains strong ties with community physicians in the Puget Sound area, many of whom have trained at Children's.

The 208-bed hospital and medical center is home to more than 200 physicians and dentists, many of whom also serve as instructors a the University of Washington, as we as conducting research. Some of th finest specialists and interdisciplinary support teams answer the call when the area's children are in nee Children's offers numerous specialties, from genetics to cardiovascula surgery, as well as plastic and reconstructive surgery.

More than simply a world-class medical facility, Children's has a well-deserved reputation for being a caring, child-friendly environment where doctors and staff truly know children—because they treat only children. "Kids are different," says Katz. "They're not little adults. We really emphasize families getting involved. Families are a part of the care team."

Partnerships with other leading medical and research facilities ensure patients will receive exceptional care both now and in the future. In an effort to speed the development of new treatments for cancers and provide integrated cancer care, the Fre Hutchinson Cancer Research Cente

ıe University of Washington, and ·hildren's have formed the Seattle ·ancer Care Alliance (SCCA). A new ıpatient unit for the SCCA, which ıcludes pediatric marrow transplant atients, opened in July 1999. Other ·ew partnerships with health care pro-ıders throughout the Puget Sound ·ea and a number of regional spe-ıalty clinics exist to provide a broader ınge of medical treatment to children ıroughout the Pacific Northwest.

Children's has recently completed comprehensive research planning ·rocess. This strategic effort will help osition Children's as a national ·ader in improving the health care ·r all children. Cancer, Genetics and)evelopmental Conditions, and ·nmunology and Infections Diseases ave been identified as the research ·reas that will serve as the focus of ·s expanded research program.

Medical research, though, is only ·art of the challenge when treating ·hildren. The Children's Clown Care ·nit, a program of Children's Recre-tional Therapy Playroom, adminis-·rs healing humor to patients, with ·uch procedures as red nose trans-·usions, and plate-spinning platelet ·sts. In efforts such as these, the hos-·ital adds a caring touch to what can ·ften be sobering medical practice.

Partner with the Community

Such a high level of patient care would not be possible without ·he tremendous support from the ·ommunity—its donors, volunteers, ·nd guild members. Children's ded-

icated army of volunteers contributes thousands of hours of service to the hospital every year. The responsibility for raising private funds is shared by two organizations: Children's Hospital Foundation and Children's Hospital Guild Association.

Both organizations work to increase community understanding, provide support and commitment to the hospital, and ensure that no child is denied medical care, regardless of a family's financial situation. The hospital provides more than $20 million each year in uncompensated care to families unable to pay.

Children's emphasizes community involvement in other ways, such as collaborations on campaigns for safety standards on drowning prevention, bicycle helmets, sudden infant death syndrome, and shaken baby syndrome, among others. The hospital also offers a Web site at www.seattlechildrens.org for the benefit of people wanting to know more about its services.

Children's will continue to emphasize development of regional facilities, bringing care closer to home for the families it serves, while delving into research to help speed the development of new treatments for all children.

Treating the children of the Pacific Northwest with the best care available, Children's Hospital and Regional Medical Center offers invaluable benefits to patients and families, staff, and the community as a whole. The comforting fact remains, "No one knows children like Children's."

Treating the children of the Pacific Northwest with the best care available, Children's Hospital offers invaluable benefits to patients and families, staff, and the community as a whole.

For more than 80 years, The Boeing Company has set the standard of leadership in the aerospace industry. Boeing led in the transition from wood-and-canvas to metal airplanes. The company also led in the transition from the piston era to the jet age. It pioneered in space exploration. And now, as an integrated provider of an expanding range of aerospace products and services, Boeing is pushing both the envelope of flight and the envelope of value for customers and partners around the globe.

Today's Boeing is a true global company, with customers, suppliers, and partners around the world. The company has the unique capability of providing globally integrated aerospace solutions to complex customer requirements, whether it is in providing the highest level of technical support to an airline's airplanes in dozens of countries around the world, or in providing an advanced airborne early warning and control system to an allied nation that draws upon the company's combined expertise in space, defense, and aviation.

Each day, Boeing exports some $72 million of goods and services to customers worldwide, sends approximately 4,650 shipments of spare parts to airline customers worldwide, and sells more than $1 million over the Internet at Boeing.com, putting the company in the top five of all Web commerce sites.

Boeing is also the world's biggest builder of military aircraft and NASA's largest contractor. For example, in the next 24 hours, some 335 satellites put into orbit by Boeing launch vehicles will pass overhead and some 6,000 Boeing military aircraft will be on guard with the air forces of 27 countries and with every branch of the U.S. military. The company's capabilities and related services also include helicopters, electronic and defense systems, missiles, rocket engines, launch systems, and advanced information and communication systems.

Development and Growth

William E. Boeing, the company's founder and a Yale University-trained engineer, operated according to a simple philosophy: Always insist upon the best, even if that means having to do it yourself. As a young man in Seattle, Boeing became interested in sailing. Finding he didn't particularly like any of the sailing yachts that were for sale, he bought a shipyard to build one. When he became hooked on a new hobby—flying—he converted the shipyard into what would become the greatest airplane design and manufacturing operation that the world has ever known.

The first Boeing plane, a seaplane christened the Bluebill, completed its first flight on June 16, 1916, and the company was incorporated a month later. Boeing's first advertising slogan, Built Where the Spruce Grows, reflected the advantages of the company's location in Seattle. Not only was there an abundance of the right kind of timber for making

The Boeing Company and Seattle have shared a mutually rewarding relationship for close to a century.

irplanes, but there were also plenty
›f skilled woodworkers in the
›eattle area.

Through the decades that have
ollowed, Boeing has gone on from
vood to metal and an increasing
ıse of composites; from seaplanes
o airplanes; and from jet planes to
pace-faring vehicles and exceed-
ngly complex space-based systems.
Today, more than 11,000 of the
vorld's fleet of approximately 13,000
etliners are Boeing airplanes. Daily,
nore than 3 million passengers will
ɔoard some 42,300 flights on Boeing
etliners, carrying them to nearly
:very country on Earth.

Boeing isn't simply an airplane manufacturer. The company also leads the way in the aerospace industry as well.

›eattle-Based Strength

In a fast-moving and interconnected global business environment, 3oeing continues to be well served ɔy having Puget Sound as its world ıeadquarters and the center of its :ommercial airplane operations. While access to cheap and plentiful supplies of timber is no longer a factor, Boeing benefits from Seattle's position as one of the world's great ıubs in the movement of goods by and, sea, and air. There are the great quality-of-life benefits to having a ıome base in the majestic Pacific Northwest as well.

In Seattle, as well as in other places where the company has large numbers of people, Boeing and its employees are extremely active in the community. Boeing is the largest grant maker in the Pacific Northwest. In 1999, contributions of cash and in-kind services by Boeing and its employees exceeded $96.6 million, supporting education, health and human services, arts and culture, and civic and environmental programs around the United States, with about 44 percent of the total going to recipients in Washington state.

Through a volunteer group called the Bluebills—named after the first Boeing airplane—Boeing employees, retirees, and families donate their time and expertise to hundreds of nonprofit organizations in the Puget Sound area. Boeing volunteers serve on boards of directors, as chairs of fund-raising for capital campaigns, and as one-on-one volunteers.

Boeing has an enduring set of values. These include a commitment to the highest standards of quality and safety, to design and engineering excellence, to the highest level of customer knowledge and support, and to community involvement and improvement. The future is bright. "We hope you will be along for the ride," Phil Condit, Boeing chairman and CEO, said in the company's 1999 annual report. "There is no limit to this flight."

Virginia Mason Medical Center

Virginia Mason Medical Center (VM is large enough to provide innovative, one-stop health care, yet small enoug that people experience the friendliness of an old-fashioned, patient-centere hospital and associated clinics. Virginia Mason staff work together ver closely in a Team Medicine℠ approach that makes the medical center unique i the Northwest. Team Medicine is a vital part of VM's ability to deliver integrated health care that results in superior outcomes.

This philosophy of exceptional, patient-centered care goes back to Virginia Mason's opening in 1920. Its founders had a then-radical idea: offer patients a single place to receive comprehensive medical care for virtually any medical need—all from providers employed by one organization.

A Focus on Service

The original Virginia Mason Hospital opened at the corner of Spring Street and Terry Avenue with six physician offices and 80 beds. The hospital was named after the daughters of James Tate Mason, M.D., and his partner John M. Blackford, M.D.

Today, VM boasts nearly 400 doctors and more than 5,000 staff, with primary and specialty care in 45 different medical, surgical, and diagnostic fields. VM's nursing staff consistently rates "exceptional" in *The Best Hospitals in America* and many VM doctors are listed in *The Best Doctors in America.* VM is a place where specialists and primary care physicians work as a team to offer high-quality service, care, and patient outcomes.

Each year, VM has more than one million outpatient visits and about 16,000 hospital patients. In addition to a 336-bed hospital, VM features a network of 16 clinics and occupational medical facilities; a philanthropic foundation; the Bailey-Boushay House, a nursing residence and day health center for people living with AIDS; and the internationally recognized Benaroya Research Institute at Virginia Mason.

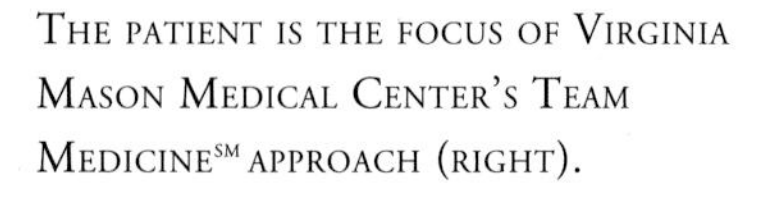

The patient is the focus of Virginia Mason Medical Center's Team Medicine℠ approach (right).

With the Benaroya Research Institute at Virginia Mason, patients benefit from clinical trials and the latest research breakthroughs (left).

A Leader in Research

Patients benefit from VM's pioneering research, with hundreds of clinical trials and patient-based research projects taking place annually. This is in keeping with VM's mission "to advance the quality of medical care through research from bench to bedside." The research center offers dedicated clinical research units for cancer, arthritis, and diabetes.

Virginia Mason's Benaroya Diabetes Center is the oldest and largest diabetes care program in the Pacific Northwest. More than 10,000 patients receive their diabetes care each year through VM. The Heart Institute the Cancer Institute, and the Cosmetic Services Group at Virginia Mason also are among its areas of excellence.

In VM's Heart Institute, patients receive comprehensive, integrated services, from diagnostic examinations and treatment to rehabilitation. The Heart Institute is a major referral source for Northwest hospitals and boasts a catheterization lab that is a training center for physicians nationwide. While patients receive leading-edge treatment in all types of cardiac care, the areas of electrophysiology and cardiac surgery are particularly noteworthy.

The Cancer Institute offers more than 29,000 patient treatments each year. VM focuses on a patient-centered, team approach to combating cancer. Ongoing research provides patients with the latest cancer-fighting techniques and drugs, as well as an entry into prevention studies conducted

ith the National Cancer Institute
ıd the Fred Hutchinson Cancer
esearch Center.

The Cosmetic Services Group
VM is unique in the region. The
oup is comprised of physicians from
fferent medical and surgical depart-
ents, including dermatology, oph-
almology, otolaryngology/facial
astic surgery, and plastic and recon-
ructive surgery. The doctors work as
dedicated team to enhance the physi-
l appearance of patients, whether
e desired procedure is due to an
cident, illness, birth defect, or
ersonal preference.

Virginia Mason's hyperbaric
ıamber is the only facility of its kind
the Northwest for emergency treat-
ıent of carbon monoxide poisoning,
noke inhalation, gas embolism,
ecompression sickness ("the bends"),
nd necrotizing infections. Hyper-
aric oxygen therapy also is used to
eat certain chronic, nonhealing
ounds. The chamber is available
4 hours a day, and VM serves as the
)ivers Alert Network headquarters
or the Northwest.

xceptional Care

These services represent only a few of the reasons that VM receives
egional recognition as a pioneer in
ınovative practices. Its history exudes
umerous firsts, including being the
rst to use insulin to treat diabetes
1923) and the first hospital west of
he Mississippi River to do an electro-
ardiogram (1927). VM also was first
n the region to provide short-stay surgery (1974), establish a nurse-midwifery program (1979), use an insulin pump for diabetes (1980), and establish a bilingual, multi-Asian clinic within a full health care system (1997).

Along with the focus on the latest advances in patient care and research, VM counts medical education as a core part of its mission. The medical center offers the oldest residency program in the state. Each year, more than 4,000 future physicians inquire about and apply for 36 first-year residency positions in five accredited programs: general surgery, internal medicine, diagnostic radiology, anesthesiology, and transitional year. In addition, VM offers 15 to 20 on-site educational opportunities each year for its phy-sician and nursing staff to enhance their personal and professional growth.

For more than 80 years, patients have received exceptional care at Virginia Mason Medical Center. The center has experienced tremendous growth, yet maintains its warmth and team focus, which translate into extraordinary service and care.

Virginia Mason has comprehensive, innovative services in many areas, including cancer, general and vascular surgery, cosmetic services, heart care, and diabetes.

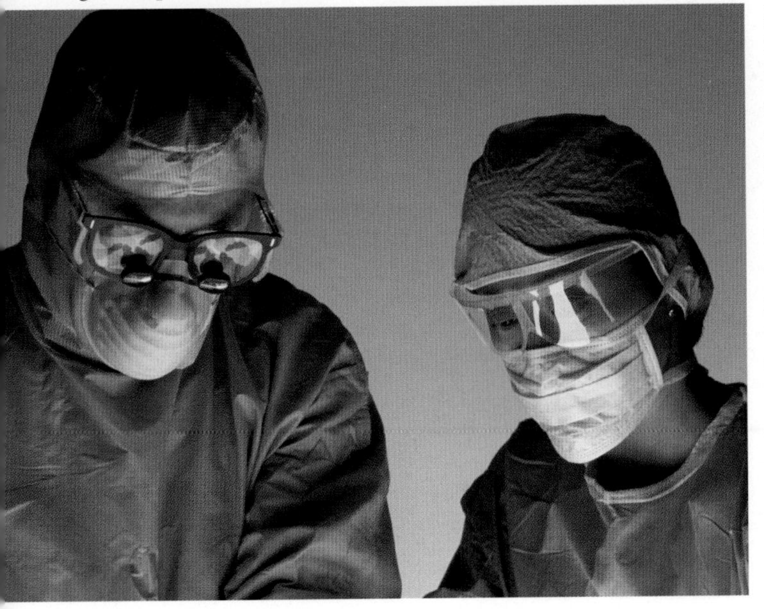

Most of Virginia Mason's specialists have regional, and sometimes national, reputations in their areas of expertise.

SEATTLE'S PREMIER MUSICAL THEATER PLAYHOUSE, THE 5TH AVENUE THEATRE, OPENED IN 1926 AS A VENUE FOR VAUDEVILLE AND SILENT PICTURES. THE THEATER'S CHINESE-INSPIRED DESIGN—A DIVERSION FROM OTHER THEATERS' PREVAILING FRENCH, SPANISH, AND ITALIAN INFLUENCES—REPRESENTED A SIGNIFICANT ARCHITECTURAL SHIFT FROM THE STANDARD PRACTICE OF THE TIME. ● THE 5TH AVENUE THEATRE SET A PRECEDENT IN INTERIOR DESIGN IN KEEPING WITH Seattle's reputation as the gateway to the Orient. Under the supervision of architect Robert C. Reamer, the interior was modeled after three of ancient imperial China's most stunning architectural achievements: the Forbidden City, the Temple of Heavenly Peace, and the Summer Palace.

Reamer possessed such a genuine concern for authenticity in design that he employed the renowned Gustav F. Liljestrom, chief designer for the S&G Gump Company of San Francisco, a decor firm famous for its hotel and theater interiors. Together, they created The 5th Avenue—a theater whose decor is nearly as breathtaking as the quality of entertainment presented within its walls. Perhaps the most stunning feature of the interior is the nearly exact replica of the dome from the throne room of the imperial palace in Beijing's Forbidden City.

The theater's magnificent chandelier, located in the center of the ceiling and twice the scale of the original in Beijing, is a symbolic representation of the emperor's right to rule China through his attainment of perfection. The theater's great, coiling dragon has five toes—each representing an evil spirit he must overcome; when the fifth spirit was subdued, a pearl issued forth from the dragon's mouth, here presented as the Pearl of Perfection chandelier.

Restoration of a National Treasure

In 1978, The 5th Avenue Theatre closed its doors and seemed destined for the same fate as the Metropolitan and the Orpheum, two of Seattle's once splendid, now demolished theaters. But in 1979, a combination of 43 companies and business leaders set the stage for the theater's rebirth. Their mission was to provide firm financial footing that would restore one of the grandest, most ornate theaters in the city. In essence, the group knew the historic theater would serve to enhance Seattle's diverse cultural community.

The group formed The 5th Avenue Theatre Association, a nonprofit organization responsible for the restoration of the national historic treasure and for the successful presentation of theatrical productions. That year, the association underwrote a $2.6 million loan for the renovation.

The entire renovation was completed without local, state, or federal funds, setting a precedent for theater nationwide. In 1980, The 5th Avenue Theatre became the first facility in the Pacific Northwest to receive the

CLOCKWISE FROM TOP:
THE INTERIOR OF THE 5TH AVENUE THEATRE IS MODELED AFTER THE THRONE ROOM OF THE FORBIDDEN CITY IN BEIJING. BUILT IN 1926, THE THEATER WAS ORIGINALLY A VAUDEVILLE HOUSE AND REIGNED AS ONE OF SEATTLE'S PREMIER MOVIE PALACES FOR MORE THAN 50 YEARS.

AFTER LAUNCHING THE THIRD NATIONAL TOUR FROM THE 5TH AVENUE IN 1992, *THE PHANTOM OF THE OPERA* RETURNED FOR A SIX-WEEK, SOLD-OUT ENGAGEMENT IN 2000.

COILED IN THE DOME OF THE 5TH AVENUE THEATRE'S INTERIOR IS AN IMPERIAL DRAGON, "THE GREAT, BROODING GENIUS OF THE PLACE," AS DESCRIBED IN THE THEATER'S OPENING NIGHT PROGRAM IN 1926.

▼ DICK BLSHER

eritage Conservation and Recre-
ion Service Achievement Award
om the Department of the Interior.

As the result of the renovation, e theater emerged as Seattle's newest ome for national touring shows. At e renovation dedication ceremony n June 16, 1980, Helen Hayes—lled the First Lady of the American heater—declared, "The 5th Avenue heatre is a national treasure."

In 1989, The 5th Avenue Musical heatre Company was established a resident, nonprofit theater com-any to produce and present the best usical theater entertainment in a ibscription series. Offering a mix f new and classic musical theater, e series enjoys the support of nearly),000 subscribers, making The 5th venue one of the largest subscrip-on-based theaters in the nation.

In the past two decades, the eater has played host to such leg-nds as Katharine Hepburn, Robert oulet, Carol Channing, Richard Iarris, Mickey Rooney, Tommy 'une, and Lauren Bacall, to name few. Since its restoration, The 5th venue Theatre has produced or resented nearly 100 productions r more than 3,000 performances. ome 5.5 million people have attended, ith average annual attendance at pproximately 300,000.

reserving the Musical heater Art Form

ducational outreach is a major part of The 5th Avenue Theatre's ork. Adventure Musical Theatre a key component of its youth out-each initiative. Designed to travel to elementary schools, the program introduces kindergarten and elementary school children to the American musical theater through the performance of original musicals in an imaginative and interactive way. Adventure Musical Theatre complements the Special School Matinee Program, which provides reduced-price performances for students in grades three to 12.

Since its inception in 1995, Adventure Musical Theatre has staged 267 performances for more than 75,000 students in Washington schools. Preserving and developing the American musical as an art form are central to the theater's mission, including expansion of the library of American musicals through the creation of new works.

The 5th Avenue Musical Theatre Company has played a key role in the development of several new musicals, including a musical adaptation of James Michener's *Sayonara* in 1993; *Annie Warbucks*, which toured nationally for 15 weeks prior to opening off-Broadway in 1993; the Arthur Kopit and Maury Yeston *Phantom*, which has enjoyed more than 80 productions since 1991, including several international companies; and *Jekyll and Hyde* in 1995, which toured nationally prior to opening on Broadway in 1997, and continues to tour nationally and internationally into the 21st century.

In addition to presenting national tours and producing its own musicals, The 5th Avenue Theatre makes its facilities available for concerts, lectures, films, and nonprofit events. With such a rich history in Seattle and a future full of promising productions, The 5th Avenue Theatre is truly a jewel in the area's artistic scene and a shining example of how a historic theater can be reinvented to serve its community

▸ CHRIS BENNION

▸ CHRIS BENNION

▸ CHRIS BENNION

CLOCKWISE FROM TOP LEFT:
STAGE AND SCREEN STARS MATTHEW ARKIN AND GREGORY HARRISON THRILLED AUDIENCES IN THE 1999 5TH AVENUE PRODUCTION OF THE MUSICAL CLASSIC *GUYS & DOLLS*.

BROADWAY NOTABLES MARC JACOBY AND PATTI COHENOUR STARRED IN THE 5TH AVENUE'S 1999 PRODUCTION OF THE TONY AWARD-WINNING *THE SECRET GARDEN*. (PICTURED: PATTI COHENOUR, PIERCE CRAVENS)

THE 5TH AVENUE'S SPLASHY 1996 PRODUCTION OF *SINGIN' IN THE RAIN* BROUGHT SEATTLE'S FAMED RAINFALL INDOORS, WITH MORE THAN 700 GALLONS OF WATER "RAINING" ONTO THE STAGE AT EACH PERFORMANCE.

THE MAGNIFICENT TOURING PRODUCTION OF RODGERS AND HAMMERSTEIN'S *THE KING AND I* PLAYED THE 5TH AVENUE IN 1997 WITH HAYLEY MILLS AS MS. ANNA.

BEGINNING AS A SMALL DOMESTIC SHIPPE OF FRESH FLOWERS MORE THAN A HALF CENTURY AGO, AIRBORNE EXPRESS HAS GROW INTO A $3 BILLION GLOBAL TRANSPORTATION AND LOGISTICS COMPANY. IT IS A FORTUN 500 MEMBER AND THE THIRD-LARGEST DELIVERY CARRIER IN AMERICA. ● AIRBORN JOINS THE FORCES OF 24,000 EMPLOYEES, 15,000 DELIVERY VEHICLES, 16,000 DRO BOXES, 310 STATIONS, AND 1.3 MILLION SHIPMENTS PER DAY. IT SERVES MORE THA 500,000 customers in more than 200 countries.

The company has survived in a fiercely competitive market, where industry giants Federal Express and United Parcel Service (UPS) adopt higher profiles. Despite the marketing machines and promotional efforts of these two larger companies, Airborne continually increases its market share and enjoys brand loyalty greater than that of any of its competitors.

A History of Growth

The company started as two entities. The first was Airborne Flower Traffic Association of California, founded in 1946. The second was Pacific Air Freight, founded in Seattle in 1949 by Holt W. Webster, a former U.S. Army Air Corps officer. Webster's operation transported perishable goods to and from Seattle. The two companies grew separately for decades, oblivious to their common future.

In 1968, the two companies merged and established headquarters in Seattle. The Airborne Express name was coined in 1976. The air express industry was still comparatively young in the 1970s; overnight delivery was a premium service, used only by a small portion of the market that could afford the price when speed was a must. A key development was the 1980 purchase of the Wilmington, Ohio airport. Airborne's leaders sensed the need for complete control of airline operations, including owning and operating fleets of aircraft and trucks.

Armed with its own infrastructure, Airborne immediately began the task of developing a national distribution network. To keep customer costs down, the company invested in quality, used aircraft, including DC-8s, DC-9s, and YS-11s.

With a long history of involvement, Airborne's leaders reflect the company's stability and patience. Robert S. Cline has been Airborne's chairman and chief executive office since 1984. He has been with the company in one capacity or anothe since 1965, serving as vice president of finance, senior vice president of finance, vice chairman, and chief financial officer.

Robert G. Brazier, president and chief operating officer, has been pa of the company since 1963. He was promoted to vice president, operations

BEGINNING AS A SMALL DOMESTIC SHIPPER OF FRESH FLOWERS MORE THAN A HALF CENTURY AGO, AIRBORNE EXPRESS HAS GROWN INTO A $3 BILLION GLOBAL TRANSPORTATION AND LOGISTICS COMPANY. IT IS A FORTUNE 500 MEMBER AND THE THIRD-LARGEST DELIVERY CARRIER IN AMERICA.

DESPITE THE MARKETING MACHINES AND PROMOTIONAL EFFORTS OF LARGER COMPANIES, AIRBORNE CONTINUALLY INCREASES ITS MARKET SHARE AND ENJOYS BRAND LOYALTY GREATER THAN THAT OF ANY OF ITS COMPETITORS.

1968. He served as vice president, omestic division operations until e became president in 1978.

Philosophy of ilored Service

While its competitors spend millions on advertising and promoon, Airborne focuses on customer rvice with flexible, cost-effective, ate-of-the-art solutions. It's an pproach described admiringly as he antithesis of mass marketing" y authors Michael Treacy and Fred Viersema, who highlighted Airborne their best-selling business book *he Discipline of Market Leaders.*

Part of Airborne's success derives om a focus on corporate customers nd business-to-business deliveries. om Branigan, Airborne's public lations manager, points out that 5 percent of Fortune 500 companies e Airborne clients.

Airborne's business focus means e company doesn't have to worry bout thousands of individual clients ho want single deliveries. Instead, e firm seeks out the customers it ants to serve. Airborne employs national account managers to serve the largest clients with the most complicated needs, such as Xerox and IBM.

ROBERT S. CLINE HAS BEEN AIRBORNE'S CHAIRMAN AND CHIEF EXECUTIVE OFFICER SINCE 1984. HE HAS BEEN WITH THE COMPANY IN ONE CAPACITY OR ANOTHER SINCE 1965, SERVING AS VICE PRESIDENT OF FINANCE, SENIOR VICE PRESIDENT OF FINANCE, VICE CHAIRMAN, AND CHIEF FINANCIAL OFFICER.

In the case of Xerox, the company needed deliveries to arrive at specified times. Airborne analyzed delivery routes and developed a system of identifying Xerox packages in order to speed shipments to specific locations. Airborne also used multiple modes of transportation, depending on specific service needs.

Continuing Commitment to Innovation

Airborne's latest innovation is Airborne@Home, a unique delivery option for catalog companies and E-tailers. The company promises to deliver shipments from businesses to residences across the United States with an unprecedented combination of speed and economy.

Customers using Airborne@ Home give Airborne shipments destined for residential delivery. Airborne takes it from there, transporting the shipments to the city of their final destination. They are then turned over to the U.S. Postal Service for delivery to the customer's doorstep. The Airborne@Home service reinforces Airborne's commitment to its business customers, providing them another way to profitably ship their goods and adapt to an ever changing marketplace. Airborne's success is due to a deeply considered approach to customer service that industry experts describe as customer intimacy. With the company's long-standing commitment to service, its continued success is sure to follow.

In the Puget Sound region, the Benaroy name has been synonymous with quality real estate development for nearly hal a century. After Jack Benaroya established the Benaroya Company in 1956, i flourished as it built such projects as the Parkway Plaza shopping center a Southcenter; the 6100 Building Gift Mart and Design Center Northwest i Seattle; and engineering offices for the Boeing Company's 747 program i Everett. Through the years, the Benaroyas became best known for their development of several million square feet of industrial space in the Kent Valley, and for their award-winning business parks in Seattle and Bellevue.

In 1984, in a feat of remarkable timing—just ahead of what would be a decade-long tailspin in real estate—the Benaroyas startled industry watchers by selling their entire portfolio.

Larry Benaroya subsequently took over management of the family's enterprises. For the next 10 years, he managed the company's assets in publicly traded securities and made private-capital investments in growing local ventures. He also continued to track real estate trends, watching for the right time to reenter the Pacific Northwest real estate market.

In 1995, The Benaroya Company burst back onto the real estate scene by purchasing extensive holdings in the Greater Seattle area. Soon, the local real estate market began to ru hot, and the legend of the Benaroyas' near-prophetic timing grew.

An Agile Decision Maker

The Benaroya Company's expertise and ample capital allow it to move quickly. Its 1995 purchase of Metropolitan Park—a 700,000-square-foot campus in the Denny Triangle area of downtown Seattle, which included a development site for a third building—was accomplished in just 21 days, meeting the seller's need for speed.

In the next 16 months, the company also acquired the 21-story Park Place Building in downtown Seattle, and established its presence on the Eastside with a series of acquisitions in Bellevue, Redmond, and Bothell.

The Benaroya Company's agility is also evidenced by its successful leasing and development activities. Since 1996, in addition to developing the third Metropolitan Park Tower the company has developed 2.5 million square feet of industrial space, primarily in the Kent Valley. All of its developments began without

© 2000 Stewart Hopkins

© 2000 Stewart Hopkins

Clockwise from top:
The Benaroya Company reentered the Seattle real estate market in 1995 with the acquisition of Metropolitan Park East and West Towers—and the development site for construction of a third tower. The new Met North tower, completed in 2000, was fully leased during construction.

In 1997, The Benaroya Company acquired 10 buildings and a development site along the Canyon Park high-tech corridor in Bothell.

The Benaroya Company acquired Northup North in Bellevue in 1996, a complex of five Class A office buildings in a parklike setting.

re-leasing, and were leased prior to ɔmpletion.

And in a town-pleasing move, 'he Benaroya Company recently urchased an imperiled Seattle landıark, the former Rainier Brewery, ɔr Tully's Coffee Corporation. The opular Tully's leased the facility for s new headquarters and roasting lant, and Seattle has retained some f its favorite industrial architecture.

Market Leader

Today, The Benaroya Company's holdings extend from Seattle ɔ Auburn, and from the Bothell-.edmond Tech Corridor to the heart f Bellevue. The company employs staff of 45, including professionals xperienced in the acquisition, develpment, management, and leasing f commercial property.

Because its activities have long een centered in the Puget Sound ɛgion, the company's powerful maret presence is supported by a keen nderstanding of historic area trends. 'he Benaroya staff takes pride in its bility to maintain long-term relationhips with its clients by meeting the hanging needs of current tenants nd anticipating the requirements of ew tenants. "We've always done qualy work, and we're proud of our ɛputation," says Larry Benaroya.

Tradition of Philanthropy

The Benaroya family has been involved for many years in focused hilanthropy. When maestro Gerard Schwarz raises his baton before the Seattle Symphony, it is in Benaroya Hall, the new, world-class venue completed in 1998 with the help of a $15.8 million lead gift from the Benaroya Foundation. And when researchers at Virginia Mason Medical Center delve into the mysteries of diabetes and other autoimmune diseases, they work under the roof of the state-of-the-art Benaroya Research Institute, named in recognition of a $3.5 million contribution from the Benaroya Foundation. These and numerous other charitable, cultural, educational, and medical organizations have benefited from the Benaroyas' long-standing commitment to the well-being of their home community.

THE BENAROYA COMPANY'S ROOTS ARE IN THE DEVELOPMENT OF QUALITY WAREHOUSE FACILITIES. THE COMPANY CONTINUES TO BE ACTIVE IN THE KENT VALLEY, WHERE IT HAS DEVELOPED MORE THAN 10 MILLION SQUARE FEET OF INDUSTRIAL SPACE (LEFT).

THE BENAROYA COMPANY RECENTLY ACQUIRED THE FORMER RAINIER BREWERY. THE SEATTLE LANDMARK IS NOW HOME TO TULLY'S COFFEE CORPORATION'S HEADQUARTERS AND ROASTING PLANT (RIGHT).

THE BENAROYA COMPANY ACQUIRED THE PARK PLACE BUILDING IN 1996. THE 21-STORY BUILDING IS IN THE HEART OF SEATTLE'S CENTRAL BUSINESS DISTRICT, ADJACENT TO FREEWAY PARK AND THE UNIVERSITY STREET I-5 ON-RAMP.

THE EXPRESSION "FAMILY BUSINESS" IS A INADEQUATE DESCRIPTION OF BURNSTEAD CONSTRUCTION. THE COMPANY, BUILT O THE BRAWNY SHOULDERS OF FRED BURNSTEAD AND HIS SONS, RICK AND STEV BURNSTEAD, IS ACTUALLY A GENERATIONAL TRIO OF BUSINESSES UNITED BY COMMO GOALS OF QUALITY, CRAFTSMANSHIP, AND INNOVATION. ● COMMUNITIES THROUGH OUT THE PUGET SOUND REGION BEAR THE BURNSTEAD STAMP. THEY INCLUDE FAIRWA at Snoqualmie Ridge, Kensington, Timberline Ridge, and Abbey Road. In each neighborhood, the Burnsteads incorporate unique accents and design features that reinforce the company's concept of building quality homes tailored to the specific needs of individuals.

At any given time, the Burnsteads and their affiliate companies are at work on roughly 12 communities in the Puget Sound region, varying in size, scope, and cost. Known for building high-level homes in exclusive neighborhoods, the Burnsteads focus the same level of dedication to quality and attention to detail on their mid-level and multifamily neighborhoods. The company also provides prospective buyers and realtors a comprehensive overview of each neighborhood under development on its Web site at www.burnstead.com. This all-encompassing dedication to the art of building has not gone unnoticed. The Burnsteads are consistently among the leading Marketing and Merchandise Excellence (MAME) award winners, sponsored by the Master Builder's Association of King and Snohomish counties.

THE BURNSTEADS INCORPORATE UNIQUE ACCENTS AND DESIGN FEATURES INTO EVERY HOME AND NEIGHBORHOOD CONSTRUCTED—WHILE ALWAYS MAINTAINING THE HIGHEST-LEVELS OF QUALITY AND ATTENTION TO DETAIL.

Building Communities

The Burnsteads are firm believers in community service. In the spring of 2000, more than 100 Burnstead employees and subcontractors worked together on a companywide effort to rehabilitate Salisbury Court, a low-income apartment complex in Kirkland that provides transitional housing for families in need. Together, volunteers painted and cleaned the complex. They also installed new fixtures and carpeting, fixed cabinets and plumbing, and developed a play area for the children. Ultimately, the volunteers' efforts resulted in 12 clean, comfortable homes.

The Burnsteads are also sponsors of United Way of King County. In fact, the company takes community involvement so seriously that it promotes 100 percent participation in community service among all its em ployees. Burnstead Construction als sponsors community events, such a Redmond Derby Days, and acts as contributing sponsor to local school and parks activities.

Founder Fred Burnstead is a prominent figure in the Puget Soun community, serving on the board o directors of the Redmond Chambe of Commerce, United Way Eastsid Community Council, and the Boar of Education Foundation of the Mas ter Builders Association. Burnstead is also a past president of the Maste Builders Association of King and Snohomish Counties, as well as a pas director of the National Associatior of Homebuilders.

In 1999, Burnstead received one of the highest honors of his long caree The University of Washington (UW) inducted him into its Construction Hall of Fame. "Fred Burnstead has built more than 4,500 homes in thi area over four decades," says Dr. Saeed Daniali, chairman of UW's construction management program "He's had a big influence on the indus try, is very involved in the community and has made significant contributions to education. He's definitely a Hall of Famer."

FOR ALMOST 40 YEARS, PACIFIC SCIENCE ENTER HAS THRILLED CHILDREN AND ADULTS ALIKE WITH HANDS-ON EXHIBITS THAT NLIGHTEN AND ENTERTAIN. FROM ROARING DINOSAURS TO EXOTIC BUTTERFLIES TO ONE F THE ONLY IMAX MULTIPLEXES IN THE NATION, THE CENTER'S WIDE RANGE OF TTRACTIONS CONTINUE TO PLEASE VISITORS OF ALL AGES. ● WITH OVERALL ANNUAL TTENDANCE AVERAGING MORE THAN 1 MILLION, AND MEMBER HOUSEHOLDS EXCEEDING ,000, the center enjoys a high egree of exposure. Planners and rogram managers work to comne permanent exhibits with unique ecial events, ensuring that the nter remains a vital and vibrant traction for spectators throughout e Seattle area and beyond.

▸ ERIN HOGAN

DESIGNED BY MINORU YAMASAKI, THE PACIFIC SCIENCE CENTER HAS BEEN DELIGHTING BOTH CHILDREN AND ADULTS SINCE 1962.

Famed History

he center opened on October 22, 1962, the day after the closing of e 1962 World's Fair. The distinctive esign by architect Minoru Yamasaki atures five buildings surrounding hite arches rising above a court of flecting pools.

During the World's Fair, the cenr served as the U.S. Science Paviln. When that famous exposition osed, the Science Pavilion was given ew life as the private, nonprofit acific Science Center. On opening ay, the center drew one paid admison—but many more would follow.

Subsequent years saw a host of mous exhibits. In 1969, the center ecame the first science center in the ation to display moon rocks from nar expeditions. In 1970, the crew f Apollo 12 visited the center. And 1975, Pacific Science Center began hat would become a beloved tradion of laser light shows.

IMAXimum Entertainment

n 1979, the center showed its first IMAX film in the restored Eames heater. The film, *To Fly*, sent viewrs on a dizzying journey through e clouds. IMAX—short for maxiium image—produces a format ree times larger than standard 70illimeter film, producing a sensation f total immersion. Ever improving MAX technology has spawned a eries of visual milestones since the ebut of *To Fly*, including the introuction of IMAX 3-D.

In 1998, Pacific Science Center pened a second theater, the Boeing IMAX Theater, creating one of the only IMAX multiplexes in the United States. Recent films shown at the center include *Everest*, a visit to the top of the world; *Into the Deep*, a spectacular underwater adventure; and *Fantasia 2000*, the first-ever featurelength animated IMAX film.

A Variety of Exhibits

In 1984, the center opened one of its most popular exhibits ever: *Dinosaurs*, featuring nine moving, roaring, robotic dinosaurs placed in a tropical setting. The exhibit was installed permanently in 1992.

In December 1998, the science center opened a new wing, the Ackerley Family Exhibit Gallery. It features two permanent exhibits: Insect Village, a hands-on entomology exhibit, and the Tropical Butterfly House, which features free-flying, exotic butterflies from around the world in a year-round tropical environment of 80 degrees and 80 percent humidity.

In addition to permanent exhibits, the science center sponsors annual events, such as a model railroad show and a bubble festival. Center program planners also work to schedule the most popular touring exhibits as they emerge. In 1995, the center attracted more than 1 million visitors for the first time—a feat that has been repeated in the intervening years, demonstrating the center's resilience and readiness to embark on a fifth decade in the new millennium.

▸ DANI WEISS

▸ NICK GUNDERSON

THE ACKERLEY FAMILY EXHIBIT GALLERY FEATURES BOTH THE INSECT VILLAGE AND THE TROPICAL BUTTERFLY HOUSE (LEFT).

SINCE ITS OPENING IN 1984 THE *DINOSAURS* EXHIBIT HAS BECOME ONE OF THE CENTER'S MOST POPULAR ATTRACTIONS (RIGHT).

THE SON OF A BOATBUILDER, JOHN F. BUCHA HAS ALWAYS PRIDED HIMSELF ON CRAFTSMANSHIP AND PERFECTION, AND THE COMPAN HE FOUNDED IN 1961 REFLECTS HIS IDEALS. JOHN F. BUCHAN HOMES HAS BUILT A REPUTATIC FOR QUALITY WORK AND EXACTING PRECISION THAT HAS TURNED A ONCE SMALL OPERATIC INTO A COMPANY THAT NOW TOPS $100 MILLION IN ANNUAL REVENUE ON A REGULAR BASI ● "HE STARTED IT SWINGING THE HAMMER HIMSELF," SAYS KATIE BUCHAN-WHITENE daughter of the founder and now president of sales and marketing. "He has great vision."

John F. Buchan Homes products can be found throughout the Seattle region and Greater Puget Sound. The company's projects have stretched from Gig Harbor in the south to Blaine in the north, just below the U.S.-Canada border. Its planned communities, floor plans, and marketing department regularly win awards from housing organizations, as well as the Sales and Marketing Council. Annually, John F. Buchan Homes completes approximately 500 closings. Many are presold before construction is complete—a reflection of the company's coveted products.

The Buchan Look

Currently, as in the past, the company constructs condominiums and office buildings, but the Buchan specialty is single-family residences, ranging in price from $180,000 to $3 million. The purchaser selects from a spectrum of designs and features, frequently requesting customized additions and upgrades.

Each home showcases the Buchan look, which is marked by steep-pitched roofs, artful mixtures of brick and stone, and overall quality. These added features have made the company popular enough that its homes are frequently listed by name in resale transactions—an uncommon distinction in the industry. "We are lucky to have a market share and a brand identity," says Buchan-Whitener.

The company's focus on excellence stems from its philosophical concept of homes as true living space in the classical tradition of commu nities such as Florence, Rome, and Paris. Buchan builds for longevity, believing that a home should be more than the sum of its parts, and is a structure that contains and shapes a family's life.

Earning Loyalty

One of the company's mottoes—Loyalty Is Earned—is reflected in the number of customers who hav purchased multiple Buchan homes and say they would accept no other Crucial to this success is in-house service. Virtually every aspect of th home ownership equation can be found within the company. John F.

CLOCKWISE FROM TOP RIGHT:
EACH HOME SHOWCASES THE BUCHAN LOOK, WHICH IS MARKED BY STEEP-PITCHED ROOFS, ARTFUL MIXTURES OF BRICK AND STONE, AND OVERALL QUALITY.

THE COMPANY'S FOCUS ON EXCELLENCE STEMS FROM ITS PHILOSOPHICAL CONCEPT OF HOMES AS TRUE LIVING SPACES IN THE CLASSICAL TRADITION OF COMMUNITIES SUCH AS FLORENCE, ROME, AND PARIS.

JOHN F. BUCHAN HOMES HAS BUILT A REPUTATION FOR QUALITY WORK AND EXACTING PRECISION THAT HAS TURNED A ONCE SMALL OPERATION INTO A COMPANY THAT NOW TOPS $100 MILLION IN ANNUAL REVENUE ON A REGULAR BASIS.

Annually, John F. Buchan Homes completes approximately 500 closings. Many homes are presold before construction is complete—a reflection of the company's coveted products.

uchan Homes operates its own rokerage, employs its own sales and iarketing staff, and oversees every age of design. In addition, a full-me architectural staff handles all lanning and evaluation duties.

In a changing market, the com-any has shown the ability to adapt) shifting forces. For many years, s efforts were limited to higher-end, ıburban, single-family homes. In ıe mid-1990s, Buchan diversified, reating divisions for entry-level omes and multifamily construction.

The strategy has borne fruit in terms of company growth. In 1994, revenues were $38 million, about one-fourth of what they are today. One project illustrating the new face of Buchan is Carrara Condominiums, a 58-unit complex on Queen Anne Avenue in the heart of Seattle. The units are long on smart detail, with recessed architectural lighting, large transom windows, European-style cabinetry, and granite countertops. Even as John F. Buchan Homes branches into the realm of downtown urban villages, the Buchan tradition of high-quality, single-family construction has taken another step. The new community of Issaquah Highlands, a few miles east of Seattle, features a series of residences that call to mind the old-style homes built in downtown Seattle after the turn of the century, complete with wraparound porches and pillared entryways—the sort that inspire casual observers to suggest that they don't build them like that anymore.

But Buchan does build them that way. The list of features for new Issaquah Highlands homes includes individual brick and stone detailing for several different plans, covered front porches, and six-panel entry doors. Inside, the floors are finished with Swedish oak and the windows are fully wrapped with wood. The master bedrooms are equipped with walk-in closets and luxurious soaking tubs. Everywhere, the stamp of quality asserts itself.

Still a Perfectionist

Even after decades in the business, Buchan is still an active participant in company projects, as meticulous as ever. He has been known to stroll through completed developments—some that have already sold and closed—and spot small imperfections. Buchan has walked up to front doors and introduced himself to surprised occupants as the builder, and then asked for permission to correct the problem. Says Buchan-Whitener, "He is still a perfectionist."

ESTABLISHED IN 1968, OVERLAKE CHRISTIA CHURCH IS A NONDENOMINATIONAL, EVANGELICAL CHURCH BUILT ON 27 ACRES A FE MINUTES FROM MICROSOFT IN REDMOND. NOW IN ITS FOURTH DECADE, THIS REGIONA CHURCH HAS NEVER LOST SIGHT OF ITS MISSION—TO HELP INDIVIDUALS AND FAMILIES GRO IN THEIR RELATIONSHIP WITH GOD AND TO MAKE A DIFFERENCE IN THE WORLD. THIS FOCU ON FAITH, FAMILY, AND COMMUNITY HAS BEEN AT THE HEART OF OVERLAKE'S GROWTH FRO a congregation of 23 members to one of the Northwest's largest churches, with weekly attendance reaching 6,300 people.

Through the years, Overlake has found many unique ways to reach out to the Seattle area. Its free, Broadway-style, holiday musical productions draw more than 30,000 people each year. Special Delivery, Overlake's transitional home for single mothers (also a United Way agency), has assisted more than 3,000 pregnant women and helped connect nearly 150 children with adoptive parents.

The church has also produced eight prime-time television programs, including the 1995 Emmy Award-winning "Spirit of Christmas." Weekly morning services are broadcast live through both radio and the Internet, and the church offers a variety of free classes in social service areas such as divorce recovery, marriage counseling, parenting, and addiction recovery. Overlake's new gymnasium is now open to local schools, as well as to nearby office workers in search of lunchtime exercise.

OVERLAKE CHRISTIAN CHURCH'S NEXT GENERATION, 5,000-PLUS-SEAT FACILITY, A NEIGHBOR TO REDMOND'S WILLOWS RUN GOLF COURSE, TRIPLED THE CAPACITY OF ITS FORMER CHURCH BUILDING.

Diversity and Growth

The balance of its contemporary style and traditional values has given Overlake a personality of its own, marked by a diverse congregation that embraces all ages and ethnic groups. The church's effort to promote diversity is highlighted by its establishment of a number of on-campus international churches that include Chinese, Iranian, Hispanic, Filipino, and Japanese fellowships. The church also helps support more than 50 missionary families around the world.

The popularity of Overlake's approach to "church" has encouraged the establishment of Overlake-style congregations throughout the Puget Sound area. Eight independent satellite churches now reach out to thousands of people each week, including those in the inner city of Seattle.

A New Church Home

Overlake's growth led to the building of its new, 250,000-square-foot complex in Redmond. The first service in the 5,000-plus-seat audito rium was held on Thanksgiving Ev 1997. The building's total capacity— including classroom, office, and ad ditional meeting space—is 10,000 people.

The new campus replaced the church's previous meeting site, whe Pastor Bob Moorehead shepherded the church's growth, both spiritual and numeric, for more than 25 years In 1998, Dr. Rick Kingham, a pastc in Denver for 20 years and a found ing member of the international Promise Keepers organization, becam Overlake's senior pastor. Kingham' style and warmth have captured the hearts of the Overlake Christian Church family as it enters its fourth decade of service to God, the Seattl area, and the world.

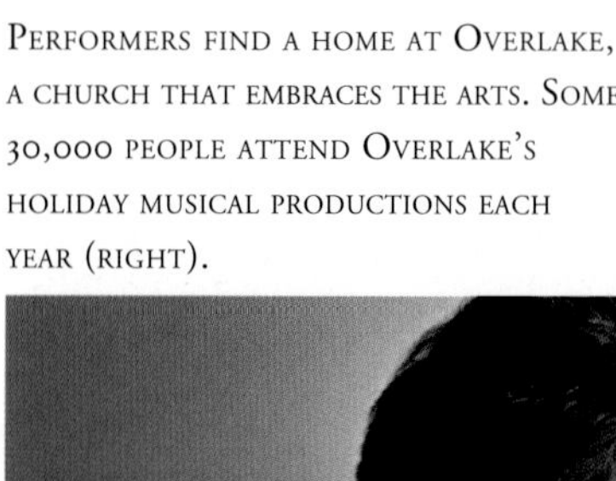

NELLIE HARRIS DIRECTS OVERLAKE'S SPECIAL DELIVERY MINISTRY TO SINGLE MOMS. MORE THAN 3,500 BABIES AND THEIR MOTHERS HAVE BEEN ASSISTED BY THIS CHURCH-SUPPORTED, UNITED WAY AGENCY (LEFT).

PERFORMERS FIND A HOME AT OVERLAKE, A CHURCH THAT EMBRACES THE ARTS. SOME 30,000 PEOPLE ATTEND OVERLAKE'S HOLIDAY MUSICAL PRODUCTIONS EACH YEAR (RIGHT).

JERRY BERG

© JIM CORWIN

1970–1985

- 1971 Sabey Corporation
- 1971 Torero's Mexican Restaurants
- 1971 Starbucks
- 1972 Gene Juarez Salons & Spas
- 1973 City University
- 1975 The Ackerley Group
- 1976 Dilettante Chocolates
- 1977 Quality Business Systems
- 1980 Christian Faith Center
- 1980 Pinnacle Realty Management Company
- 1982 Attachmate Corporation
- 1982 Fran's Chocolates
- 1983 Sandusky Radio
- 1983 Costco Wholesale

FOUNDED IN 1971 AS A GENERAL CONTRACTO SABEY CORPORATION HAS EVOLVED INTO A TOTAL FACILITIES PROVIDER THAT OFFE SITE ACQUISITION, COMPLETE DESIGN AND CONSTRUCTION SERVICES, AND DEVELOPMEN AS WELL AS PROPERTY MANAGEMENT. IN ADDITION TO ITS ROLE AS A LEADING DEVELOP SERVING THE COMMERCIAL AND INDUSTRIAL SECTOR IN THE PACIFIC NORTHWEST, SAB HAS RECENTLY BECOME A WORLD LEADER IN PROVIDING BUILDINGS THAT MEET TH unique technical requirements of mission critical Internet facilities.

Sabey has designed and built a series of Internet campuses under the name Intergate. Intergate campuses meet the requirements for multiple fiber providers, massive electrical power, heavy floor and roof loads, and space for generators and fuel tanks that these specialized tenants need to operate 24 hours a day, seven days a week, 365 days a year. Intergate Seattle, Sabey's flagship facility, is a 12-building campus housing more than 2 million square feet of Web hosting, telecom, colocation, and office space, and is the largest multi-tenant Internet campus in the world.

Sabey continues to expand the reach of its services by establishing Intergate campuses across the country. Besides Intergate Seattle, the company has two campuses in Los Angeles and one in Denver. Sabey is looking at additional locations in the San Francisco Bay Area, San Diego, Phoenix, and on the East Coast. Sabey's tenant list represents the top companies in the Internet industry.

"As a total facilities provider, we pride ourselves on giving our clients the greatest speed to market possible," says Laurent Poole, Sabey's COO. "Give us the opportunity to do what we do best: take care of all the details necessary to get the job done right and in the shortest amount of time. That level of service, combined with our track record, has propelled our company to its current status as the world leader in colocation facilities."

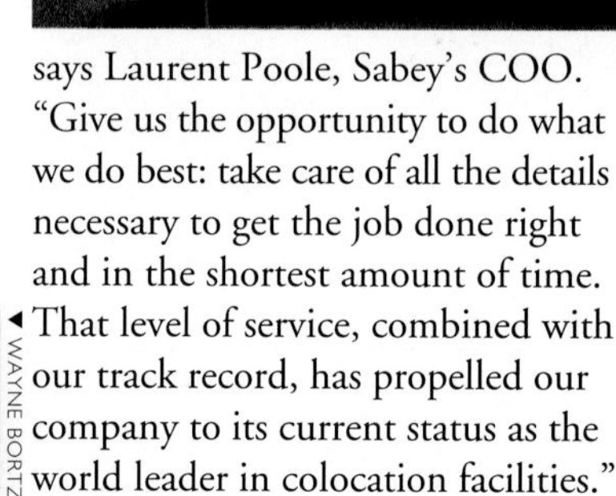

Sabey is well positioned to serve the Internet industry through expertise gleaned from years of building high-technology facilities for Boeing's military division, as well as the experience it has gained as a premier builder for the major biotech companies in the Pacific Northwest.

Sabey is a company with its foundation built on trust, tenacity, passion, and common sense, along with a proven track record of delivering facilities under the most strenuous deadlines. Clients know that Sabey has the expertise, experience, and creativity needed to get the job do on time and within budget.

Identifying ways to turn underutilized real estate into successful developments—and at a lower per square-foot cost—is another of Sabey specialties. A combination of visio construction expertise, and experien is required not only to understand what is possible, but also to comple projects cost effectively. A team of in-house architects, engineers, and craftsmen use technological experti combined with creativity, to increa a structure's value and usefulness.

Services Offered

Sabey offers uncanny responsiveness to clients who need comple facilities constructed in short time frames. A good example is Exodus Communications' Seattle II site in South Seattle, where Sabey completed a 60,000-square-foot colocatio

CLOCKWISE FROM TOP:
SABEY CORPORATION HAS DESIGNED AND BUILT A SERIES OF INTERNET CAMPUSES UNDER THE NAME INTERGATE. INTERGATE WEST IS PART OF THE 2 MILLION-SQUARE-FOOT INTERGATE SEATTLE CAMPUS, THE LARGEST INTERNET CAMPUS IN THE WORLD.

THE *SEATTLE POST INTELLIGENCER* (P.I.) HEADQUARTERS, LOCATED ON ELLIOTT AVENUE, FEATURES THE ROTATING P.I. GLOBE, WHICH SABEY RESCUED FROM ATOP P.I.'S PREVIOUS HEADQUARTERS AT FIFTH AVENUE AND WALL STREET.

DAVID A. SABEY IS THE FOUNDER AND CEO OF SABEY CORPORATION.

WAYNE BORTZ PHOTOGRAPHY

INTERGATE WEST IS LOCATED ON A HILLSIDE OVERLOOKING THE REST OF THE 12-BUILDING INTERGATE SEATTLE CAMPUS.

cility in 60 days, or the 40-acre)xbow complex that Sabey built for ıe Boeing Company. Boeing needed 647,000-square-foot structure built in o days. This was an enormous buildıg project that included extra reuirements such as a specialty "black" efense plant. The facility was designed ɔr use as a top-secret engineering and ıanufacturing plant for the F-22A ghter and B-2 stealth bomber. Sabey ompleted the project on time and ithin budget.

Sabey preserved a bit of Seattle's istory when it refurbished the *Seattle 'ost-Intelligencer* (P.I.) building at 'ifth Avenue and Wall Street near he downtown area. While retaining ıe art deco character of the old buildıg, Sabey breathed new life into the tructure, the interior of which now ɔrms a giant atrium that opens to kylights three stories above the ground loor. Today, the building is home to Group Health Cooperative, a national HMO model. In the renovation proess, Sabey saved the giant, illuminated P.I. globe, moving it to the new Seattle P.I. headquarters the firm built for the newspaper on Elliott Avenue.

As one of the largest biotech developers in Seattle, Sabey has built, owns, and manages more than 300,000 square feet of lab space, including the facilities of Cell Therapeutics, Inc., PathoGenesis, Smith Kline Beecham, and Biomembrane Institute. Sabey has expertise in the special construction, environmental, and management considerations for these technical projects.

A Passion for Community

Behind all that the company does lies a passion for community. Dave Sabey, the founder and CEO of Sabey Corporation, considers himself lucky to be a native Seattleite. "The Pacific Northwest has been good to me," he says. "It's pretty cool to have been born and raised in an area that you love, and enjoy a career there. I will be forever grateful for that."

Sabey's gratitude is more than just talk. In 1990, his company built the world-class Goodwill Games pool, which is one of the best swimming and diving facilities in the country. The site has hosted numerous competitions, including the 2000 U.S. Olympic diving trials.

Sabey used his personal persuasiveness in discussions that led the Goodwill Games to the area. In another example of his outside-the-dots thinking, Sabey—attending those meetings with U.S. maps—would point to Seattle and the Pacific Northwest, far from New York and the bustling cities of the East Coast. Then, he would bring out a globe and show a different perspective—Seattle, in the middle of the globe between New York and the Pacific Rim.

"The world is changing," Sabey says. "Are we going to sit back and let the world change us, or are we going to get out in front, and use the forces at play to slingshot us where we want to go? That's the kind of the thing that motivates us: watching Seattle become the San Francisco of the Northwest, moving from being just another nice city to a world-class city. That's pretty exciting stuff."

▲ PATRICK BARTA

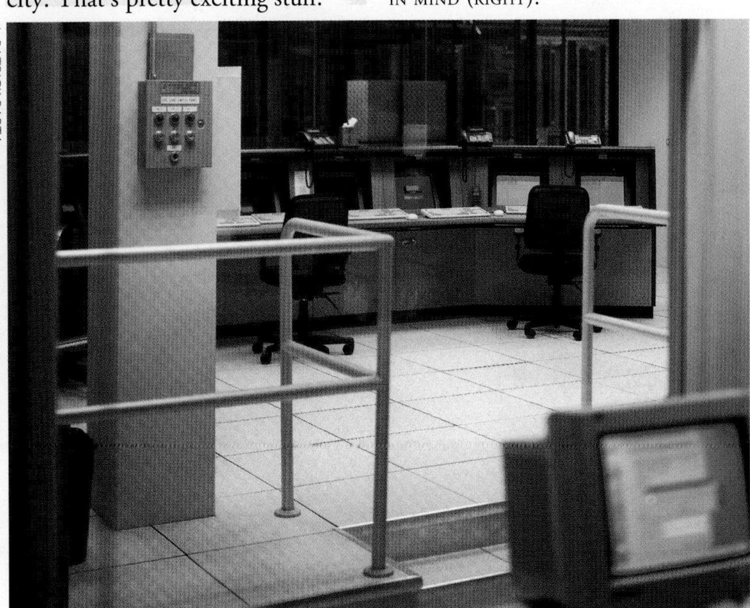

GENERATOR SETS LIKE THIS TWO-MEGAWATT UNIT ARE JUST ONE OF THE MANY BACKUP SYSTEMS USED TO KEEP INTERGATE TENANTS UP AND RUNNING 24 HOURS A DAY, SEVEN DAYS A WEEK, 365 DAYS A YEAR (LEFT).

SABEY'S INTERGATE CAMPUSES ARE DESIGNED WITH FIBER, POWER, SECURITY, AND REDUNDANCY REQUIREMENTS OF MISSION CRITICAL INTERNET FACILITIES IN MIND (RIGHT).

Torero's Mexican Restaurants

The story of Torero's Mexican Restaurants began in 1967 in Cuautla, Jalisco—a small town in Mexico. Teodoro "Ted" Rodriguez was 20 then. Cuautla was his hometown, but times were hard and his family was poor. His father was a farmer, but the growing season was always short, usually followed by seven or eight months with no rain. Rodriguez wanted to leave Mexico. "In my generation, everybody started coming to the United States—the land of dreams," Rodriguez says. His first stop was San Francisco, where he started out as a busboy and dishwasher in an Italian restaurant, learning and observing as he worked.

"I dreamed about having a little place—only my wife and I," Rodriguez says. "I always had the dream to get a store and to get my own business, but I never thought I would grow this much." He reached the state of Washington in 1975, and began to work for friends and relatives in the restaurant business.

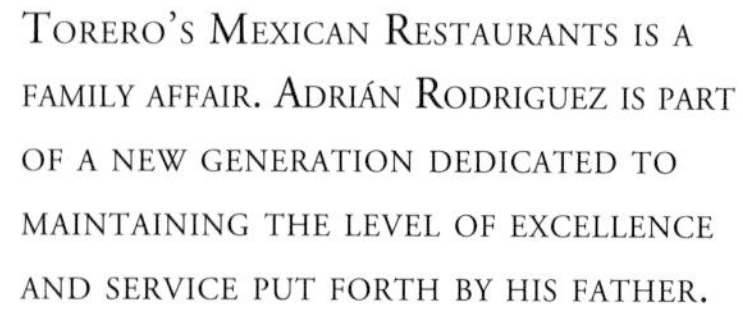

Torero's Mexican Restaurants is a family affair. Adrián Rodriguez is part of a new generation dedicated to maintaining the level of excellence and service put forth by his father.

A Family Success

The business has since expanded, while remaining in the Rodriguez family. Rodriguez's children work in the chain, as do members of the extended family.

Torero's now operates eight restaurants and *taquerias*: in Renton, where Ted Rodriguez's children, Adrián and Verónica, manage the restaurant along with Ramón Sanchez; at a second Renton location, managed by Raúl and Blanca Rodriguez; in Seattle, on Broadway East, managed by Maria and Andrés Rodriguez; in Bellevue, with Ricardo and Laura Rodriguez; in Federal Way, with Zully Villa, Dulce Casanova, and Mario Casanova; in a *taqueria*-style restaurant at the Crossroads Mall in Bellevue, managed by Daniel and Livier Rodriguez; at Lake Forest Park, where Daniel Rodriguez Jr. and Yadira Rodriguez serve as managers; and at the Sea-Tac Mall, managed by David Moreno.

The secret of success at Torero's is still the combination of food and service provided at these restaurants which are known for treating customers with a personal touch. In a 1995 restaurant review, *The Seattle Times* gave Torero's high marks. "The Rodriguezes bring a warmth, efficiency and consistency to food, décor and service," the review notes. "Diners can count on a tasty meal with good service in a casual setting."

Ted Rodriguez is a celebrity in his home base of Renton, where Torero's operates its corporate offices. In 1997 the city's Chamber of Commerce named him Citizen of the Year, thanking him for his work on behalf of the community. In that arena, Rodriguez is tireless. He is always difficult to reach because he's usually helping someone else, whether he's volunteering at senior centers, providing food to low-income families, or donating to local service clubs.

"We feel like when God gives you something, you have to share your profits with the community," says Rodriguez. "The more you give, the more the community will give you back."

Founder Ted Rodriguez's hard work both with Torero's and within the local community earned him Citizen of the Year honors in 1997 from the Renton Chamber of Commerce.

THE SECRET OF TORERO'S IS NOT JUST THE EXCELLENT FOOD, BUT THE DEDICATION OF EMPLOYEES SUCH AS RODRIGUEZ'S DAUGHTER VERÓNICA (LEFT), AND ZULLY VILLA AND DULCE CASANOVA (RIGHT).

roadening Horizons

At the time of his Citizen of the Year nomination, Rodriguez had lready formed a friendship with Ralph Iunro—then secretary of state for the ate of Washington—who quipped nat Rodriguez should be nominated s Citizen of the Century. The friendnip was built during Rodriguez's fforts to develop Washington's first ster-state relationship with Jalisco— is birthplace. Rodriguez counts Iunro and former Governor Mike owry, who supported the creation of ne sister states, among his friends. He lso accompanied current Governor Gary Locke on a recent international nission to Mexico.

Rodriguez is treasurer of the board f directors of Centro Mexicano of the State of Washington and is president of the Washington-Jalisco Sister-State Association, two nonprofit entities that develop educational and cultural exchange programs to support the Hispanic community. He is also a member of the Rotary Club in Renton and a board director of the Renton Community Foundation.

In addition to Rodriguez's direct involvement in community oriented activities, he has sponsored projects that support one of his primary goals, promotion of Hispanic culture in Washington State. He has sponsored such events as Mexico Week in Washington, Fiestas Patrias, and the Cinco de Mayo Festival. Rodriguez is a prime sponsor of *Destinos*, a local cable television program produced in collaboration with Seattle Central Community College.

Rodriguez recently widened his horizons to include radio, acquiring Promocions sin Límite and Radio Amistad 2000—two enterprises that have expanded his presence in Hispanic media. He serves as president of both companies.

Rodriguez's efforts and the support of his relatives and loyal employees have made Torero's one example of success achieved through hard work and dedication. The enterprise that Rodriguez founded more than 20 years ago represents not only a significant contribution to the economy of the region, but also a cultural expression that Torero's customers can appreciate and enjoy every day.

RODRIGUEZ'S EFFORTS AND THE SUPPORT OF HIS RELATIVES, SUCH AS DANIEL AND YADRIA RODRIGUEZ, AND LOYAL EMPLOYEES HAVE MADE TORERO'S ONE EXAMPLE OF SUCCESS ACHIEVED THROUGH HARD WORK AND DEDICATION.

IMAGINE A COZY STOREFRONT IN SEATTLE FAMOUS PIKE PLACE MARKET. STEP INSIDE THIS UNIQUE STARBUCKS STORE AND TH AROMA OF ROASTED COFFEE BEANS WILL DRAW YOU IN FARTHER. STARBUCKS BEGA ROASTING AND SELLING ITS OWN COFFEE BEANS HERE IN 1971. BUT IT WAS HOWAR SCHULTZ WHO HAD A VISION TO PROVIDE CUSTOMERS WITH NOT ONLY GREAT COFFE BUT ALSO A GREAT EXPERIENCE. AFTER JOINING THE COMPANY IN 1982 AS DIRECTOR O retail operations and marketing, Schultz traveled to Italy and had an epiphany as he wandered the streets, stopping at espresso bars along the way. Coffee in this environment was more than just a beverage; it was a social and cultural bridge.

"As I watched, I had a revelation," Schultz wrote in his 1997 biohistory of Starbucks, *Pour Your Heart Into It: How Starbucks Built a Company One Cup at a Time,* published by Hyperion. "The connection to the people who loved coffee did not have to take place only in their homes, where they ground and brewed whole-bean coffee. What we had to do was unlock the romance and mystery of coffee, firsthand, in coffee bars. The Italians understood the personal relationship that people could have to coffee, its social aspect. I couldn't believe that Starbucks was in the coffee business, yet was overlooking so central an element of it."

Starting a Coffee Revolution

Schultz returned to Seattle with a new idea of what was possible for Starbucks. When you step inside any Starbucks store today, no matter where you are in the world, you get a glimpse of that idea. Beyond the temptation of roasted coffee, Starbucks offers customers a dizzying array of wonderful beverages to match any mood—choices range from a straight shot of espresso to a cool, creamy Frappuccino® blended beverage. The baristas deliver these drinks with an unparalleled blend of expertise and familiarity. The seating area offers a comfortable spot that becomes a home away from home. In fact, for many people, Starbucks has transformed their relationship with coffee. It's no wonder that the Starbucks Experience evokes such passion in local residents.

Of course, for Starbucks the phrase "local residents" is beginning to take on a new meaning. With thousands of retail locations spanning the glob the Starbucks Experience that starte with one Seattle store is now readil accessible to millions of customers in a growing number of countries around the world. Global expansion started with Japan in 1996. Since the Starbucks has continued its expansion into a total of 19 international markets—Hawaii, Singapore, the Philippines, Thailand, Taiwan, the United Kingdom, New Zealand, Malaysia, Beijing, Kuwait, South Korea, Lebanon, Shanghai, Hong Kong, Dubai, Qatar, Australia, and Saudi Arabia. As of 2000, Starbucks signed an agreement to enter continental Europe and develop retail stores in Switzerland. While growth is an important goal, Starbucks hasn't minimized its commitment to its 40,000 partners, as employees are called.

People with Passion

Dedication to partners has been a guiding principle that has nurtured the growth and success of Starbucks throughout its history. "The relationship we have with our people and the culture of our company are our most sustainable competitive economic advantages," says Orin Smith, president and chief executive officer.

For most customers, their only interaction with Starbucks partners occurs with the baristas in the stores. These points of contact affect what customers remember and how they form opinions. So each partner is offered a thorough training program that focuses on extensive knowledge of coffee, product expertise, and a commitment to customer service.

To ensure that everyone identifies with the company's philosophy, bot full- and part-time partners who work a minimum of 20 hours a week and meet other eligibility requirements have the opportunity to participate

THIS IS WHERE IT ALL BEGAN. THE ORIGINAL PIKE PLACE STARBUCKS OPENED IN 1971 AND BEGAN SELLING FRESH-ROASTED WHOLE BEANS TO DELIGHTED COFFEE LOVERS. NOW A SEATTLE LANDMARK, THE STORE ATTRACTS BOTH TOURISTS AND LOCALS AS THEY WANDER THE MARKET AREA.

Bean Stock, the company-wide
ɔck option plan. Another little perk:
partners are eligible for their choice
a pound of coffee or a box of tea
ch week. With efforts like these,
s no surprise that Starbucks has
en named one of the 100 Best
ɔmpanies to Work For by *Fortune*
agazine for three years in a row:
98, 1999, and 2000.

Consequently, Starbucks has built
passion for excellence among its
rtners. Each person, in every job
roughout the company, shares a
mmon vision—this passion for
cellence. The coffee buyer who
lects the highest-quality arabica
ans, the roaster who roasts the
ans to perfection, the merchandiser
ho buys the products, the barista
ho handcrafts each cup of coffee—
ch partner strives to go beyond what
expected. And it's this passion
at makes Starbucks not only an
spiring place to enjoy coffee, but
inspiring place to work as well.

Starbucks is the type of place
at consistently attracts the best
eople for all job opportunities. The
ɔmpany's extraordinary partners
eliver a potent blend of commitment
ɔt only to the highest-quality prod-
cts, but also to their communities.
arbucks strongly encourages part-
ers to make positive contributions
n a local level. On a global scale,
arbucks supports a variety of orga-
izations that benefit literacy, child-
n's welfare, AIDS outreach, and
nvironmental awareness.

haring Common Ground

Starbucks is equally passionate about the organizations with
hich it becomes involved—seeking
thers who share similar values and
assions. In 1998, Starbucks began a
int venture with basketball legend
arvin "Magic" Johnson's company,
ɔhnson Development Corporation,
n order to establish Starbucks stores
n developing urban neighborhoods.
'he first of these stores opened in
os Angeles in the Ladera Center and
reated a much-needed gathering
lace within that community. As of
Jovember 2000, additional stores
ave opened in under-served neigh-
orhoods in Harlem, New York;
eattle; Hyattsville, Maryland;
Atlanta; Chicago; San Francisco; East Lansing, Michigan; and Oakland.

Through CARE, the international aid and development organization, Starbucks designs and funds projects that improve the lives of people in coffee-origin countries. As the largest North American contributor to CARE, Starbucks has helped to establish clean water systems in Guatemala and Indonesia, develop children's education services in Kenya, and contribute toward regeneration efforts in a coffee-growing region of Ethiopia.

Starbucks also works with Conservation International to promote environmentally sound methods of growing coffee. Coffee buyers who work for Starbucks travel throughout the world—from Central America to Africa to Indonesia—looking for unique coffees that meet their high quality standards. In 1999, Starbucks began offering its customers their first shade-grown coffee—a significant product because it has minimal impact on the surrounding environment.

"Through our partnership with Conservation International, we introduced customers to a wonderful shade-grown coffee from the El Triunfo Biosphere Reserve in Chiapas, Mexico," says Mary Williams, senior vice president, Coffee. "I don't think that a lot of American consumers realize the role they play in the economy of these countries just by purchasing these special coffees. We get such pleasure and enjoyment from being able to make a difference in these farmers' lives, because they make a difference in our lives every day."

Developing New Relationships

Starbucks constantly seeks products and experiences to enhance and accompany its coffee. In 1999, Starbucks acquired Tazo Tea®, a Portland, Oregon-based company that produces authentic, premium tea products. "The chance for us to

The Starbucks Roast® is not a single roasting time limit or color; instead, it's a philosophy and a style. It's understanding and roasting each individual coffee to its optimal flavor. A wonderful selection of roasted coffees is available in both retail and grocery stores.

With style and elegance, Starbucks has brought its own version of a European-influenced café concept to several Seattle locations. Café Starbucks in Madison Park provides customers the complete line of Starbucks beverages, as well as a delicious lunch and dinner menu.

take our brand to the next level really intrigued me," says Steve Smith, founder of Tazo Tea. "And to be able to take it to that next level through someone who shares our same values and passion, to do it through Starbucks stores, is pretty tremendous." Bottled, full-leaf, and filter-bag tea is now available in most Starbucks stores.

In a further effort to enhance customers' experience, Starbucks formed a strategic alliance in late 2000 to offer *The New York Times*, one of the world's most widely read and respected newspapers, in the company's extensive network of company-owned locations in the United States. "This partnership brings together two great, well-respected brands, which we believe benefits both Starbucks customers and *The New York Times* readers," says Howard Schultz, Starbucks chairman and chief global strategist. "*The Times* has always been an important source of information for people throughout the world," Schultz adds. "The coffeehouse has always been at the center of conversation, community, and culture and the marriage of our two companies is a great way to encourage that tradition to continue within our stores."

One key element that has defined the coffeehouse experience has been music. Says Holly Hinton, music specialist, "Starbucks Music was put together in response to our customers' requests for the music we were playing in our stores. We started with mostly jazz and some blues collections, but we've discovered that we can walk out a bit further." And as the desire to expand the variety of music has grown, Starbucks made the decision to acquire Hear Music™, a company dedicated tc uncovering the wonderfully hidde world of music—the new, the old the unsigned, the treasured. This new addition will allow Starbucks to gro its in-store music programming, crea in-store listening stations, and off live performances in some locations

Growing through Grocery

A desire to reach a wider audience has taken Starbucks into grocery stores. The cool, creamy, taste of Frappuccino® blended beverage appeared in 1995, and a joint venture with Pepsi-Cola brought a ready-to-drink version of the indulgent beverage to grocery stores.

In 1996, Starbucks and Dreyer's Grand Ice Cream Inc. introduced the decadence of Starbucks® Ice Cream and Ice-Cream Bars in store

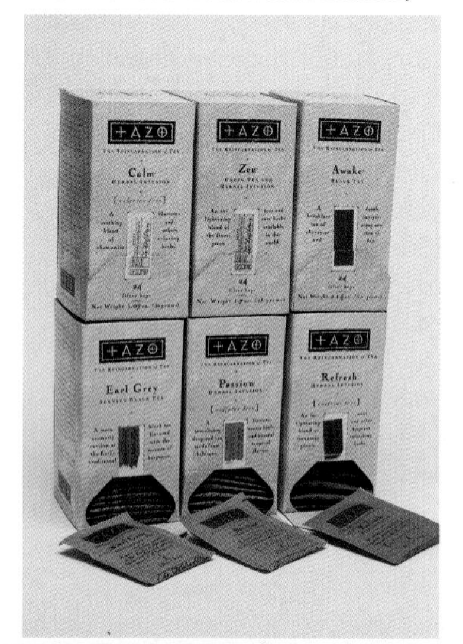

Clockwise from top left:
Tazo Tea's® passion for tea matches the Starbucks passion for coffee. Starbucks was attracted to this Portland, Oregon-based company for its innovative thinking and creativity with tea. The results can be enjoyed in filter-bag, full-leaf, or ready-to-drink, bottled form.

Starbucks baristas create hand-crafted beverages to please every palate in more than 3,500 locations worldwide.

The Starbucks Experience can be created by meeting a friend for a cool, creamy Frappuccino blended beverage, or by savoring a latté while enjoying a favorite book.

The Johnson Development Corporation/Starbucks joint venture store in the Columbia City neighborhood of Seattle provides the community with a unique gathering spot. For some, it has become a meeting place for friends; for others, it's a library. And on some occasions, the store acts as a community center.

[a]cross the United States. They began [w]ith wonderful flavors like Java Chip, [V]anilla Mocha Swirl, and Italian [R]oast, and more recently added delec[ta]ble non-coffee flavors such as Dulce [d]e Leche, Chocolate Almond Crunch, [a]nd Double Shot Chocolate.

And in 1998, in order to expedite [w]hole bean distribution to grocery [st]ores, Starbucks partnered with [K]raft Foods—combining the com[p]any's knowledge of sourcing, [r]oasting, and delivering the best coffee beans with Kraft's vast experience in marketing, selling, and distributing in this new channel.

The latest grocery milestone for Starbucks is a licensing agreement with Albertson's Inc. to establish more than 100 coffee bars in Albertson's supermarkets across the United States. This entry into the world of retail groceries opens a host of possibilities for Starbucks, since Albertson's operates more than 2,450 retail stores in 38 states.

"Americans purchase two-thirds of their coffee—whole bean and ground—in grocery stores," says Paul Davis, president, North American Operations. "These coffee bars provide a great opportunity for us to introduce new customers to the Starbucks Experience, while conveniently serving customers in a new venue."

By continuing to seek challenges and by redefining how Starbucks will become the most recognized and respected brand of coffee in the world, the Starbucks Experience has expanded beyond Seattle. It's a continuing love affair—this passion that Starbucks has ignited. As a recent Starbucks annual report states, "If we didn't feel so passionately about what we do, then we could never become the enduring company we aspire to be."

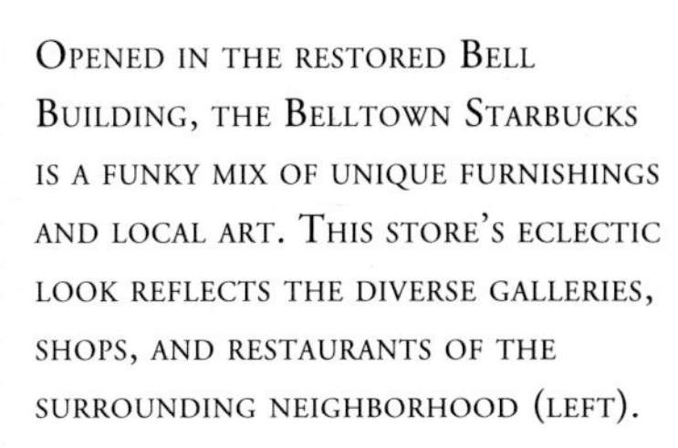

Opened in the restored Bell Building, the Belltown Starbucks is a funky mix of unique furnishings and local art. This store's eclectic look reflects the diverse galleries, shops, and restaurants of the surrounding neighborhood (left).

The Starbucks Support Center in the South of Downtown (SODO) business district occupies a building known to longtime Seattle residents as the home of Sears. Extensive renovation has created a unique office environment that reflects both the culture of the company and the personality of the building (right).

FOUNDED BY GENE JUAREZ IN SEATTL IN 1972, GENE JUAREZ SALONS & SPAS HAS BECOME INTERNATIONALLY RECOGNIZED A BEING SYNONYMOUS WITH SUPERIOR CLIENT SERVICE AND CREATIVE EXCELLENCE. INSPIRE BY ITS FOUNDER AND NAMESAKE, THE COMPANY TAKES PRIDE IN ITS COMMITMENT T MEETING THE UNIQUE NEEDS OF EACH INDIVIDUAL. ● IN FEWER THAN THRE DECADES, JUAREZ'S DRIVE AND DETERMINATION HAVE TURNED HIS COMPANY INT the dominant salon and spa operation in the region and a national industry leader. In 1997 and 2000, *Modern Salon* magazine named Gene Juarez America's Salon of the Year. Other industry publications, including *American Salon* magazine and *Salon Today*, have consistently given Gene Juarez high marks, and the company has appeared in the pages of *Allure*, *Town & Country*, *Vogue*, *Glamour*, and *Ladies Home Journal.*

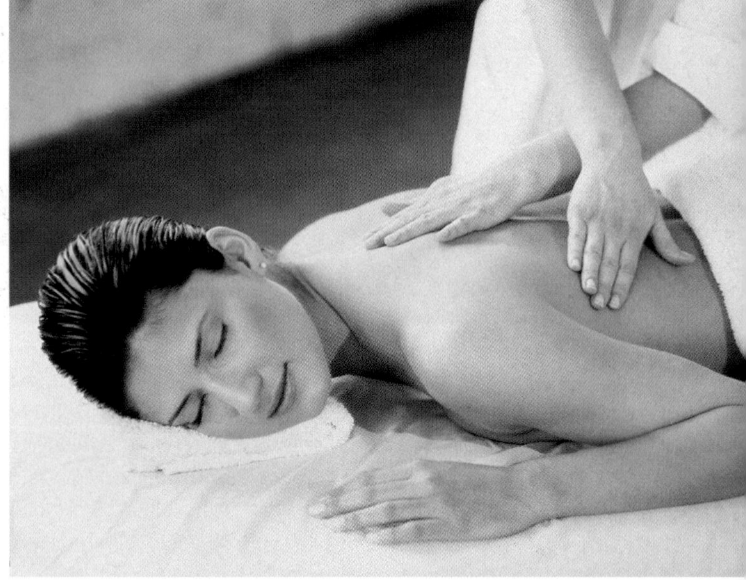

Client service and quality are the most fundamental elements of the company philosophy, as well as the bases for its continued success. In an age when people are often viewed as mere numbers and statistics, the Gene Juarez service model follows a different path—taking pride in a sincere commitment to meet the unique needs of each client.

World Class in Everything It Does

Gene Juarez Salons is composed of seven salons and spas; two of the Northwest's largest basic cosmetology schools; an advanced graduate training salon for stylists, technicians, and nail artists; a corporate office; and a 15,000-square-foot distribution center. The total number of employees exceeds 1,000, with an additional 350 students in beauty schools. Ranging from 3,000 to 24,000 square feet in size, the salons attract a total of approximately 25,000 client per week, and six of the seven salon are located in dominant positions at major mall locations.

The company recently establishe its second flagship salon in Bellevue—a 24,000-square-foot monument to luxury, comfort, and full-service wellness. Even the waiting areas are comfort zones, with couches perfec for lounging, quiet fountains, and relaxing light.

"We're really trying to be world class in everything we do," says Juarez. "My responsibility is to know what happens all over the world in all the major fashion centers. If it make us better, we're going to be there."

GENE JUAREZ SALONS & SPAS IS WORLD CLASS IN EVERYTHING IT DOES, EMBODYING LUXURY, COMFORT, AND WELLNESS–EVEN IN THE WAITING AREAS.

Emphasis on Education

Integral to the success of Gene Juarez Salons is the company's education division, comprised of two beauty schools, an advanced training salon, and an in-salon continuing education program. These systems provide the company with one of its most fundamental assets: a constantly renewing stream of trained artists, educated in the delivery of high-quality services.

The Gene Juarez Academy of ›eauty—which includes two of the ʌorthwest's largest beauty schools— ducates 20 to 25 percent of the ʌorthwest's newly licensed cosme- ›logists, according to the Wash- ıgton State Board of Cosmetology. 'he schools are state of the art, with ılonlike environments, excellent ıstructional staffs, and a curricu- ım developed by Juarez himself. Vhile many beauty schools across ıe country are struggling, both ;ene Juarez schools are operating ear capacity, servicing a high vol- me of clientele. Approximately 40 ercent of the students choose › work for Gene Juarez upon raduation.

The next step in training is the ;ene Juarez Advanced Training alon, established by Juarez to ful- ll an unmet need for higher edu- ation in cosmetology. Advanced ıstruction focuses on specific areas f expertise, allowing students to pecialize in areas such as hair cut- ıng, hair color, massage, and nail, kin, and spa body cares. Additional training and continuing education follow for students who are placed in Gene Juarez salons.

Embracing Change

Recent years have seen the expansion, evolution, and redesign of the salon and spa concept, exemplified by Gene Juarez's spectacular Bellevue facility, which brings the company's total number of newly envisioned salons to six. Large and beautiful, the new locations are complete with water features, fireplaces, hand-painted murals, aromatic essences, echoes of song, state-of-the-art equipment, and the very best salon and spa service providers. The Gene Juarez experience represents the ultimate beauty and wellness retreat, offering clients a complete range of services, plus a multidimensional sensory experience to escape, replenish, and feel beautiful.

Behind the salon and spa concept lies a thoughtful business strategy. Offering a wide range of services while maintaining a tone of luxury and quality affords opportunities for cross promotion, client retention, and, ultimately, customer loyalty. Gene Juarez's recent redesigns and expansions have been reinforced and complemented by marketing campaigns featuring celebrity hairdresser and educator Christophe Soltane and celebrity spokesperson Josie Bissett, former star of *Melrose Place.*

Juarez knows as well as anyone that his industry is in a state of permanent flux, which requires constant adjustment. "The only constant in fashion is change," he says. "If you refuse to change, then it would be stagnant. Fashion is a capitalistic expression—it has to change. You have to have the discipline to change, to be young enough in mind. That's where the creativity is. That's where the energy is. I embrace it."

Juarez believes that embracing change also means working to make a change. Gene Juarez Salons & Spas has been a regular contributor the Leukemia Society, Big Brothers, Camp Fire, and the PONCHO arts organization. Juarez also serves on the board of directors at Heritage College, an independent college in Toppenish, Washington, dedicated to serving multicultural populations.

"There's nothing greater than attitude" says Juarez. "That means a willingness to do more than others."

GENE JUAREZ SALONS IS COMPOSED OF SEVEN SALONS AND SPAS; TWO OF THE NORTHWEST'S LARGEST BASIC COSMETOLOGY SCHOOLS; AN ADVANCED GRADUATE TRAINING SALON FOR STYLISTS, TECHNICIANS, AND NAIL ARTISTS; A CORPORATE OFFICE; AND A 15,000-SQUARE-FOOT DISTRIBUTION CENTER.

THE DOORS OF CITY COLLEGE OPENED I 1973 IN SEATTLE WITH ONE PRIMARY PURPOSE: TO PROVIDE ACCESS TO QUALITY HIGHE EDUCATION, ESPECIALLY FOR SEGMENTS OF THE POPULATION NOT BEING FULLY SERVE BY TRADITIONAL MEANS. IN 1982, THE NAME WAS CHANGED FROM CITY COLLEGE TO CIT UNIVERSITY BY THE SCHOOL'S BOARD OF GOVERNORS. ● CITY UNIVERSITY'S BOAR OF GOVERNORS REVISED A STATEMENT OF GOALS IN 1991 TO GUIDE THE NEXT STAGES O the school's development. The university's principles are embodied in these goals, which read as follows: "To serve the intellectual needs and professional aspirations of its students, and to contribute to the intellectual and professional vitality of its host communities, and of society at large; to create for students the environment and programs that help to satisfy current needs and anticipate future ones; and to contribute to the preservation, transmission, and enlargement of an important segment of the common social and educational heritage; and to foster an awareness that organizations, institutions, and individuals should be committed to work toward the genuine improvement of the condition of all."

A City University Education

Each degree or certificate awarded by City University is an affirmation of the knowledge, skill, and academic attainment of the recipient. The university measures its success as an organization by the accomplishments of its graduates and their individual contributions to society.

"A City University degree stands for much more than excellence in education," says President Steve Stargardter. "It represents a wide breadth of knowledge and a firm grasp of concepts that shape today's ever changing world."

Early leaders of the university gath ered inspiration and influence from a Carnegie Commission report and the Seattle 2000 Commission. The work of those organizations informec the university's pioneering decision to focus its efforts on working adults

The university's on-campus student body, which numbers close to 6,000, consists primarily of workin adults drawn from all walks of life. Most are already established in eithe a job or a career, and have chosen a path they are preparing to follow. More than 51 percent of the students in the 1998-1999 academic year were women; more than 18 percent were members of minority groups.

City University offers a range of undergraduate programs that culminate in bachelor of science or associate of science degrees. Students are given a vast array of options, and may choose the course of study best suited to their experience, their prior learning, and the realization of thei

CITY UNIVERSITY'S STUDENT BODY, NUMBERING CLOSE TO 6,000, COMES FROM ALL WALKS OF LIFE.

THE GOAL OF CITY UNIVERSITY IS, "TO SERVE THE INTELLECTUAL NEEDS AND PROFESSIONAL ASPIRATIONS OF ITS STUDENTS, AND TO CONTRIBUTE TO THE INTELLECTUAL AND PROFESSIONAL VITALITY OF ITS HOST COMMUNITIES, AND OF SOCIETY AT LARGE."

ersonal and professional goals. Within those degrees, students may pursue one of several areas of study, including business administration, accounting, management specialty, computer systems, international studies, and marketing.

The university's graduate business and public administration programs prepare management professionals for leadership roles at local, national, and international levels. Thanks to significant enrollment, City University's graduate program was listed among the largest business schools in the nation by the American Assembly of Collegiate Schools of Business in 1998-1999.

Graduate students at City University may pursue a certificate or master of business administration degree, with an array of specialties. The university also caters to students seeking careers in education, offering master of education degree in curriculum and instruction, educational technology, or special education.

The City University faculty includes distinguished practitioners in the fields of business, education, government, health care, human services, civic and research organizations, and the legal community. They unite strong academic preparation and active professional careers in their respective fields. This combination of academic strength and practical experience is the most salient characteristic of the university's faculty, and assures the relevance, currency, and credibility of its instruction.

Since its founding in 1973, the doors of City University have remained open to anyone desiring access to a higher education.

From on-campus cafés to on-line course work, City University strives to provide an effective, high-quality educational environment.

istance Learning at Its Best

In keeping with its mission to make education convenient for all, the university has reached far beyond the limits of Seattle and the Puget Sound region, expanding to nearly two dozen locations throughout California, Washington State, and British Columbia, as well as in Germany, Slovakia, Spain, and Switzerland.

In the same spirit, the university has established an innovative and popular distance learning program, which makes degrees available through the traditional mail system and the World Wide Web. The distance learning program annually serves approximately 4,500 students throughout the world.

Students may receive their course work through the university's on-line instructional center, accessing course-specific video, audio, animation, and interactive assignments, as well as instructor notes. They communicate with instructors via E-mail, phone, regular mail, or fax. In 1997, the program garnered the attention of *Forbes Magazine*, which included City University on its Top 20 Cyber-Universities list.

University officials recognize the concerns raised by educators who wonder whether distance learning students learn as much as students receiving traditional face-to-face instruction. City University officials point to research comparing the methods, and note that distance teaching and studying can be equally effective, as long as methods and technologies that are appropriate to the tasks are used. They also note that timely teacher-to-student feedback is an important feature of distance learning.

"The learning experience at City University reflects progressiveness, with courses that blend the latest in technology with the most forward-thinking business, educational, and leadership ideals," says Stargardter.

FOUNDED BY BARRY ACKERLEY IN SEATTL IN 1975, THE ACKERLEY GROUP IS TODAY A NATIONALLY RECOGNIZED ENTERTAINMEN AND MEDIA FIRM WITH MORE THAN 2,000 EMPLOYEES SPREAD ACROSS SIX STATES. FRO ITS TELEVISION AND RADIO BROADCASTING DIVISIONS TO ITS OUTDOOR ADVERTISIN AND SPORTS ENTERTAINMENT VENTURES, THE COMPANY IS COMMITTED TO PROVIDIN QUALITY, SUPERIOR PRODUCTS AND SERVICES. ● IN FEWER THAN THREE DECADES, TH Ackerley Group's four divisions have grown to include 32 entertainment and media operations, all leaders in their respective fields. This remarkable success is the direct result of a company that always strives to provide the best—from customer service to the content of its productions or the management of its employees. The Ackerley Group not only sits among the elite in the radio and television markets, but also strives to always provide the resources necessary to help its businesses make an impact in the communities they serve.

THE ACKERLEY GROUP IS TODAY A NATIONALLY RECOGNIZED ENTERTAINMENT AND MEDIA FIRM WITH MORE THAN 2,000 EMPLOYEES SPREAD ACROSS SIX STATES.

The Ackerley Group's growth has been achieved primarily through acquiring undervalued or underperforming media companies and nurturing, improving, and operating them to the benefit of customers, communities, employees, and shareholders. Today, when acquiring new properties, the company targets markets where it sees an opportunity to either improve market share through clustering or enhance holdings through operating efficiencies, technological advancements, or synergistic business ventures.

THE ACKERLEY GROUP OWNS PROGRESSIVE HD MOBILE PRODUCTIONS, WHICH FEATURES NORTH AMERICA'S ONLY PROGRESSIVE FORMAT MOBILE HIGH DEFINITION PRODUCTION UNIT.

AK Media/AK Television Group

The Ackerley Group's outdoor media segment, AK Media, owns approximately 6,000 displays nationwide. AK Media is the market leader in three major metropolitan markets: Seattle and Tacoma; Salem and Portland, Oregon; and Boston and Worcester. The company also has a presence in New Jersey and New York City. AK Media provides complete, comprehensive outdoor media services, including creative development, printing, and installation.

In 1998, the company launched AK MediaPrint, the first large-format digital printing facility at an outdoor media company in the nation. The facility confers numerous advantages, including the ability to produce banners, wall hangings, and backdrops for promotional and architectural purposes, in addition to traditional billboard signage.

The 18 television stations that make up the AK Television Group reflect the company's commitment to local news and quality programming. Television is a relatively recent growth area for the company; 11 stations have been added to the portfolio since 1996.

To increase profitability and ensure a healthy local market share, The Ackerley Group focuses on stations that are geographically contiguous or in close geographical proximity. The clustering strategy creates statio groups with common management Consolidation of certain business functions and expanded local sales allow the corporation to make smal stations profitable while preserving and improving overall quality.

In 1999, the company introduced Digital CentralCasting to its statior groups, bringing a superior level of broadcast quality. The system gives The Ackerley Group the ability to deliver digital programming to mul tiple stations for slightly more than th cost of a digital system for one statior

A Full House

The Ackerley Group acquired the SuperSonics in 1983, launching the company's venture into the sport entertainment arena. The team has a long record of consistency, reaching the playoffs in 13 of 17 seasons, including 1999-2000. The team's successes also include four Pacific Division cham pionships and a Western Conferenc title that brought the Sonics to the NBA finals in 1996. In October 199 The Ackerley Group added a WNB expansion franchise, the Seattle Storm to its sports segment. The Sonics and the Storm are marketed by Ful House Sports & Entertainment,

he Ackerley Group's sports business rm. The division also produces and ells television advertising time for oth teams, as well as provides catering, executive suites, and concessions.

New Century Media, The Ackerley Group's radio broadcasting segment, perates five radio stations in the Puget Sound market. KUBE-FM is he top-rated music station in the egion, playing contemporary urban its; KJR-FM plays classic rock; JR-AM is one of the top-rated sports adio stations in the country, with a stable of popular hosts and personalities; KMBX-FM plays adult contemporary rock; and KHHO-AM transmits at KJR Sports Radio in Tacoma.

Commitment to the Community

Since beginning its community program in 1987, The Ackerley Group has donated more than $100 million in cash and in-kind contributions to numerous organizations and initiatives. In 1997, The Ackerley Group was named Outstanding Philanthropic Organization by the Puget Sound Chapter of the National Society of Fundraising Executives.

The company continues to believe that it creates a better business environment by strengthening the community. As the firm continues to grow into the future, The Ackerley Group will steadily increase its contributions to the local community, not only through charitable donations, but also through high-quality television, radio, sports, and entertainment programming.

The Ackerley Group's outdoor media segment, AK Media, owns approximately 6,000 displays nationwide (left).

The Ackerley Group acquired the SuperSonics in 1983, launching the company's venture into the sports entertainment arena (right).

The Ackerley Group not only sits among the elite in the radio and television markets, but also strives to always provide the resources necessary to help its businesses make an impact in the communities they serve.

DANA DAVENPORT, THE FOUNDER O DILETTANTE CHOCOLATES, IS A TRUE CHOCOLATIER WHOSE HERITAGE TRACES BAC THROUGH THREE GENERATIONS OF FAMILY TRADITION. HIS EXPERTISE IS BASED UPON THOROUGH LOVE OF COOKING THAT HAS FOCUSED ON CHOCOLATES AND FINE PASTRIE "CHOCOLATE WAS NAMED 'THE FOOD OF THE GODS' BY AN 18TH-CENTURY BOTANIST, DAVENPORT SAYS, SITTING AT A TABLE IN HIS SHOP ON BROADWAY IN SEATTLE' fashionable Capitol Hill neighborhood. This 'cocoa café' has become an institution in the city's culinary scene. Its pastries and the extensive menu of chocolate and mocha drinks are exceptional in every way. "Our task here has been to bring this food of the gods in all its forms to the people of Seattle and our guests that come from all over the world," says Davenport.

THE CENTERPIECE OF DILETTANTE CHOCOLATES IS ITS EPHEMERE TRUFFLE. A BITTERSWEET-ON-BITTERSWEET TRUFFLE, THE EPHEMERE TRANSPORTS CHOCOLATE LOVERS TO THEIR PERSONAL CHOCOLATE HEAVEN.

The year 2001 marks the 25th anniversary of Dilettante Chocolates, whose confections *Newsweek*—in an April 4, 1988, article—called "the best chocolate in the world." Through the years, Davenport has cooked with Julia Child on PBS, garnered national industry awards, and seen his chocolates sold in Neiman Marcus, I. Magnin, and Balducci's of New York.

A Rich Story

The Dilettante story dates back more than 100 years to Eastern Europe at the turn of the 19th century. Julius Franzen, Davenport's granduncle, was born in 1886. He began his confectionery apprenticeship in Budapest and then went to Paris for further training. Franzen was subsequently engaged as a pastry chef by the Hapsburgs in Vienna, where he was discovered by the imperial family of Russia. He received a commission as chocolatier for Czar Nicholas II and served at the Alexander Palace in St. Petersburg.

War and revolution were coming to Europe, and in 1910, Franzen, his parents, his brother, and his sister came to America. Franzen's sister married an American, Earl Remingtor Davenport—Dana's grandfather—who joined Franzen in pursuing th craft of fine confectionery.

Franzen and Earl Davenport wer lifelong friends, with Franzen sharin his recipes from the czar's kitchens. The two men continued their career as chocolatiers, consulting with eac other, and keeping very detailed records in their diaries and notebooks. Both men knew what Dana Davenport recognizes today: making candy requires the meticulous approach of a scientist, as well as the love of a great artist. "It is the most precise of all the culinary arts, and most demanding in love and respect,' Davenport says.

As a young boy, Davenport learnec the nuances of chocolate making fron his father, his grandfather, and other family members, who also participated in this grand heritage. He became caretaker of the copious notebooks kept by Franzen and Earl Davenport When Dana Davenport opened his cocoa café on Broadway in 1976, hi confections and pastries quickly became a phenomenal success.

To this day, chocoholics can be seen lining up on Broadway, waiting for a seat in Dilettante Chocolates. The store inspires romance: not a month goes by without a marriage proposal being presented at one of the tables. Management even provide complimentary chocolates and champagne for the occasion.

◄ DARRELL PETERSON PHOTOGRAPHY

DANA DAVENPORT, FOUNDER OF DILETTANTE CHOCOLATES, IS A TRUE CHOCOLATIER WHOSE HERITAGE TRACES BACK THROUGH THREE GENERATIONS OF FAMILY TRADITION. HIS EXPERTISE IS BASED UPON A THOROUGH LOVE OF COOKING THAT HAS FOCUSED ON CHOCOLATES AND FINE PASTRIES.

Seattle Institution

The centerpiece of Dilettante Chocolates is its Ephemere ʼruffle—the name Davenport's ˌrandfather used for his dark chocoıte truffle. A bittersweet-on-bitterweet truffle, the Ephemere transports hocolate lovers to their personal hocolate heaven.

Today, the company offers not ·nly boxed chocolates, but also its vorld-famous Ephemere Truffle auce. This rich, bittersweet ganache s used in Davenport's ice-cream undae and Coupe Dilettante, and lso forms the base of his signature offee drink, the Ephemere Mocha. And, for the fun of it, Dilettante Chocolates also makes chocolateoated almonds, espresso beans, nd dried cherries.

Dilettante Chocolates provides upport for the city's major art instiutions. For the Seattle Opera's production of Wagner's *The Ring*, Davenport was commissioned to make a new confection, which he called Rheingold—a butter-pecan toffee, dipped in chocolate, with more butter than the Rhine River had gold. For the Seattle Symphony he created the Dilettante Symphoneve Mint Truffle.

And then there is the Champagne Truffle, a ganache of chocolate, cream, butter, and Marc de Champagne, dipped in the milkiest of milk chocolates and garnished with true strawberry crystals. The Champagne Truffle was inspired by the Romanovs' tradition of offering their imperial guests a bedtime serving of champagne, strawberries, and chocolates.

Davenport loves chocolate in all its forms. "When we began in 1976, our line was predominantly bittersweet chocolate truffles when most West Coast consumers were eating milk chocolate, but the last five years have seen consumers come around to the taste of fine dark chocolate," Davenport notes. "In response to this new demand for dark chocolate, the best growers and suppliers are focusing on deeper, more complex cacao varietals. Also, there is a trend at the agricultural level to produce better-quality cacao in a more environmentally responsible way."

Davenport adds, "I knew from my grandfather how difficult the depression and war years were for cacao growers and candy makers, but this new century will be much more fun for chocolatiers everywhere. I'm excited to be a part of it."

Davenport continues to present fresh, modern creations, based on centuries of tradition. His store now offers Ephemere Port Milkshakes and the Ephemere Mocha Express—Ephemere Truffle Sauce with a shot of espresso. The signature pastry of the Broadway store is the *Rigó Jancsi*, a Hungarian dessert of chocolate genoise, chocolate mousse, and chocolate glaze. "Chocolate in all its forms" is how Davenport describes this dessert, which is also how one would describe the success of his company, Dilettante Chocolates.

The signature pastry of the Dilettante store on Broadway is the *Rigó Jancsi*, a Hungarian dessert of chocolate genoise, chocolate mousse, and chocolate glaze.

The year 2001 marks the 25th anniversary of Dilettante Chocolates, whose confections *Newsweek*—in an April 4, 1988, article—called "the best chocolate in the world."

▸ DARRELL PETERSON PHOTOGRAPHY

SINCE 1977, QUALITY BUSINESS SYSTEM HAS PROVIDED A BROAD LINE OF IMAGING SOLUTIONS, INCLUDING SALES AND SERVICE O DIGITAL, CONNECTED COPIERS AND PRINTERS; DIGITAL COLOR COPIERS AND PRINTER HIGH-SPEED NETWORK PRINTERS; DIGITAL FAX MACHINES; ELECTRONIC PRESENTATIO SYSTEMS; AND DIGITAL NETWORKING SERVICES, BOTH IN SEATTLE AND AROUND TH COUNTRY. ● THE FIRM'S PARENT COMPANY, GLOBAL IMAGING SYSTEMS, INC., IS

business with a national identity, but Quality remains a distinctly local company, with offices in Tacoma, Redmond, and Seattle. Quality's latest achievement is its designation as official document technology provider to the NFL's Seattle Seahawks.

Thinking Globally, Acting Locally

"We're part of a national organization, but our philosophy in business—unlike most conglomerates—is Think Globally, Act Locally," says Teri Dunn, Quality's president. "Every community is different, so we offer different programs," she says. "All the financial decisions run through here. We dispatch service, and inventory everything at a local level. We're really autonomous, and we're empowered to make decisions that affect our community."

Local decision making has proved to be a successful strategy for Quality. As the core operating company of Global's Northwest Group, Quality in 2000 led the charge toward a second consecutive Chairman's Trophy, awarded annually for outstanding performance as measured by revenue growth, operating income growth, growth in cash flow, return on assets, and return on investment.

"Quality has made a concerted effort to recruit, hire, and train the top talent not only from within our industry, but from outside of our industry, within the greater metro Seattle area," says Brian Landgren, senior vice president of West Coast operations. "The service organization has gone through manufacturer-provided training to assure that the company is a top-quality service performer."

TeamPower

The company's newest innovatio is its TeamPower concept—a broad-based approach to service tha harnesses the integrity, work ethic, and energy of employees working i concert with customers in a focused and productive manner. The company sends teams of marketing and

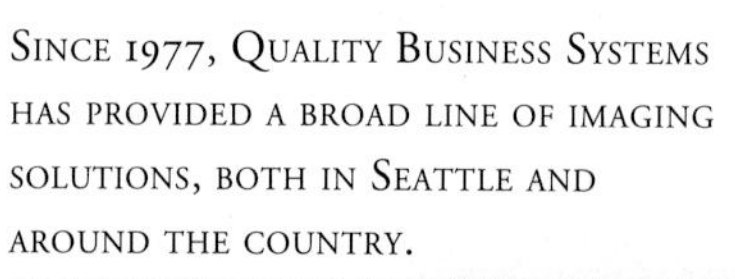

SINCE 1977, QUALITY BUSINESS SYSTEMS HAS PROVIDED A BROAD LINE OF IMAGING SOLUTIONS, BOTH IN SEATTLE AND AROUND THE COUNTRY.

chnical professionals to customers oking for innovative operating lutions.

The team begins with an overall sessment that examines document ork flow, total volume, identifica- on of current technologies, a cost nalysis, and a service and support aluation. The structure is pre- se, in keeping with the demands f prominent customers such as arborview Hospital, Overlake ospital, Seattle University, Uni- ersity of Washington, and many f Puget Sound's major law firms.

Dunn points out that Quality's bilities stretch across the United tates and beyond. "Kevin Keating, ur national accounts manager, facili- tes fully implemented systems for nore than 400 PostNet locations."

"Obviously, customer service is a g issue to us," says Service Manager om Arney. "Customer respect and putation are what I feel sell our quipment. My focus is to try to nake the salesperson's job very easy y giving our company a very good rvice reputation. That's my goal. Ve build that reputation by respond- ng to customer needs very quickly— nd once we respond, to have the aining and the parts to be able to ake care of the problem, make a ne-stop fix, and not have to return ecause we didn't carry that part or ecause the wrong person was sent."

In 2000, Quality led the charge toward a second consecutive Chairman's Trophy, awarded annually for outstanding performance as measured by revenue growth, operating income growth, growth in cash flow, return on assets, and return on investment.

The teams establish maximum equipment performance standards, setting a four-hour emergency service protocol. Technicians familiar with the needs of large organizations help customers manage the demands of multitasking and networking, while consolidating technical support needs and helping businesses operate at peak efficiency in a connected environment.

Another recent development is the establishment of the company's ecom-division. When customers need a product that Quality doesn't carry, the ecom-division's value-added service connects the business with a source already found to be reliable and supportive.

Quality's latest achievement is its designation as official document technology provider to the NFL's Seattle Seahawks.

Community Involvement

Quality's TeamPower concept doesn't stop with customer service. It extends to the workplace culture within the company. Quality encourages employees to become involved in the community by providing paid days off specifically for volunteer activities.

"It's part of our philosophy within the culture of the organization," says Landgren. "We always encourage employees very strongly to participate in volunteer organizations." A key area of community involvement is the company's use of radio time. Dunn notes that Quality is in the habit of purchasing airtime at peak hours to recognize companies, organizations, and individuals who contribute to the community. The Salute program has recognized companies and organizations such as Sudden Printing, for its efforts on behalf of the Union Gospel Mission; FreeInternet, which supports the Starlight Children's Foundation; and the Seattle Seahawks Academy. "We buy radio time and actually do a 60-second spot highlighting them in morning drive time," says Dunn.

She cites a recent example of a team—affiliated with Bellevue's Overlake Hospital—that climbed Alaska's Mount McKinley to raise money for the hospital's breast health cancer center. Quality purchased time to single out the team's efforts and recognize its goal. "That is a philosophy that we have, of trying to give something back to the community," Dunn says.

FOUNDED IN SEATTLE IN 1978, SANDUSK RADIO TODAY OPERATES FIVE RADIO STATIONS IN THE SEATTLE AREA, GATHERED IN UNIQUE SETTING UNDER ONE ROOF ON THE EASTSIDE OF LAKE WASHINGTO PRESERVING THE INDIVIDUAL IDENTITY OF EACH STATION IS IMPORTANT TO TH COMPANY, IN SPITE OF THE COLLABORATIVE TENANCY. SHARING ONLY A RECEPTIO AREA, LUNCHROOM, MAIL ROOM, AND MAIN CONFERENCE ROOM, EACH STATIO retains its own studios, office space, sales and support staff, as well as promotion departments.

Targeting Adults in the Pacific Northwest

KLSY-FM 92.5 bills its playlist as Today's Hits and Yesterday's Favorites, and enjoys a healthy audience in the crucial 25- to 54-year-old listener category. The station's high-profile morning show, *Murdock, Hunter & Alice*, provides listeners with a combination of upbeat music and entertaining features for those dealing with the ever challenging morning commute. Always looking to give back to the community, the KLSY Teddy Bear Patrol collects teddy bears to calm and comfort lost, frightened, or injured children. The KLSY Teddy Bear Patrol has been around for some 13 years, and works with the police, the state patrol, firefighters, paramedics, and hospitals throughout all of western Washington. KLSY's patrol is the largest teddy bear collection program in the United States.

KIXI-AM 880 has carved a niche for nostalgic listeners who crave adult standards that include Frank Sinatra, Tony Bennett, Barbra Streisand, Nat King Cole, Neil Diamond, the Beatles, and Johnny Mathis. The older demographic KIXI reaches provides penetration into an often overlooked market. The morning show features two of Seattle's most recognizable voices—host Jim Dai and newsman Jim Kampmann.

KWJZ-FM 98.9 has quickly become a real company success story. Operating its unique Smooth Jazz format, which fits the Pacific Northwest lifestyle perfectly, KWJZ has proved to be very popular among adults, and is becoming an increasing dominant force in the Seattle marke KWJZ produces an annual Smooth Jazz Festival, which sells out each yea and a Smooth Jazz CD project, whic has raised more than $250,000 for local charities.

KRWM is Warm 106.9 FM, Seattle's only soft adult contemporary radio station; the station featur continuous soft favorites. Well suite for at-work listening, KRWM featur Elton John, Celine Dion, Rod Stewar and the Backstreet Boys. The annua Warm Coats for Warm Kids campaig collects coats for underprivileged children each winter.

KSRB-AM 1150 is the newest addition to the Sandusky family and ha already received national recognitio it was named ABC's Affiliate Statio of the Year in 1999. KSRB's call letter

FOUNDED IN SEATTLE IN 1983, SANDUSKY RADIO TODAY OPERATES FIVE RADIO STATIONS IN THE SEATTLE AREA, GATHERED IN A UNIQUE SETTING UNDER ONE ROOF ON THE EASTSIDE OF LAKE WASHINGTON.

nd for Seattle's Rhythm and Blues—
oviding a large Seattle audience with
olid Gold Soul, featuring Diana Ross
d the Supremes, Ray Charles,
arvin Gaye, and Aretha Franklin.

inning in a Competitive Market

eattle's radio arena is a very competitive one, currently dominated
five major companies, including
ndusky. Thanks to federal legislaon easing restrictions on ownership
multiple stations, consolidation
s become a standard feature of the
dustry. Much of the company's
rategic thinking centers on the ever
ifting world of demographics and
eir relationship to advertising.

Sandusky's team of leaders always
ants to know who's listening, and
a result, their efforts to reach difrent consumer targets take a variety
forms. Vice President and General
anager Mark Kaye, Director of Sales
usan Hoffman, and Director of
arketing Scott Paine have worked
ard to create a fun and unique work
ivironment—one they feel is neces-
ry when it comes to running five
ry different radio stations.

Like other radio station groups,
andusky is constantly positioning
self in an effort to take advantage
Puget Sound's robust economy,
ıeled in large part by growth in highch industries. As one of the nation's
ıost "wired" communities, Seattle
resents Sandusky with the opportuity to pursue 21st-century marketing
chniques, combining standard broadıst spots with highly effective proıotions and full-service streaming
ation Web sites.

Seattle's affluent population and economic growth are currently coupled with an overburdened transportation system, familiar to all of the city's residents. The situation may not make commuters happy, but it means increased travel time and, therefore, increased in-car listening, which is ideal for all of Sandusky's stations.

Despite the advent of the Internet and technology, industry statistics still show radio as a dominant medium, exceeding television, newspapers, and magazines. An even more compelling statistic for advertisers is the likelihood that consumers will be exposed to radio one hour before making a purchase. On that score, radio nearly triples the exposure rate of television advertising.

The Wages of Consolidation

The decision to bring the five Sandusky radio stations together under one roof was Kaye's, and a considerable outlay was required to start Sandusky's state-of-the-art, multimillion-dollar facility. In fact, the complex has garnered industry-wide attention: the November 1999 issue of *Radio Ink* magazine lists it as one of America's 10 Best Radio Facilities. "The view of the city is enough to keep any on-air personality motivated," the magazine noted.

After searching for more than a year, Kaye located 18,000 square feet of space, which was subsequently reconfigured into engineering, studio, and office spaces. Simply connecting the cable cost $100,000, and the stations are wired with more than three miles of conduit. Digital control boards, new chairs, and state-of-the-art equipment combine to create high-quality facilities in an industry not commonly known for having posh surroundings.

The view might be nice, but it is Sandusky's dedication to providing quality programming in a variety of formats that has made it a serious player in the Pacific Northwest radio market for two decades—and counting.

Clockwise from left:
The KLSY Teddy Bear Patrol has been around for some 13 years, and works with the police, the state patrol, firefighters, paramedics, and hospitals throughout all of western Washington.

The view might be nice, but it is Sandusky's dedication to providing quality programming in a variety of formats that has made it a serious player in the Pacific Northwest radio market for two decades—and counting.

KRWM Warm 106.9 FM's Warm Coats for Warm Kids campaign collects coats for under-privileged children each winter.

As founder of Christian Fait Center, Casey Treat, along with his wife, Wendy, has built a church for new generation. He believes God is the dynamic and driving force in th lives of ordinary people looking for inspirational and practical ways to ge and stay on course with their lives by renewing their minds. Treat's passionat philosophy has inspired him to build one of the largest multicultura

nondenominational churches in the Pacific Northwest.

Christian Faith Center (CFC) provides weekly services to more than 6,000 residents in the Seattle area, and reaches an international audience through a weekday television show, *Living on Course.* Its schools provide education for kindergarten-grade 12 through Christian Faith School, and Dominion College offers a two-year biblical discipleship program.

CFC's Media Director Debera Willis attributes Treat's success to his willingness to be radical. "His goal is to make this a lifestyle, not a Sunday-only thing," Willis says.

Casey and Wendy Treat are founders of Christian Faith Center, one of the largest multicultural, nondenominational churches in the Pacific Northwest.

Reaching Out in Many Ways

Treat has authored more than 30 books and continues to cultivate all forms of media to reach people on a global scale. Christian Faith Center hosts its own Web site at www.caseytreat.org, as well as offers a multitude of books, tapes, seminars, and youth programs—all designed to build stronger families. The 46-year-old pastor and motivational speaker travels widely, pursuing his mission to pastor the Northwest, teach the nation, and inspire the world.

In 1985, the Treats also started Vision Ministers Fellowship (VMF) to teach other Christian leaders how to bring their passion for God to their roles as pastors. Today, VMF's 1,000 members gather quarterly to sharpen their leadership skills, exchange ideas, and renew ministry relationships.

By combining basic Bible teachings with unique and unconventional sermons and family services, Treat helps families achieve success spiritually, intellectually, emotionally, physically, financially, and socially. Treat challenges people to reexamine their traditional images of church as boring sermons delivered in little white buildings.

Treat asserts that church should not be a mere shot in the arm once a week to help endure another week, and is willing to apply his unconventional approach to his sermons and his outreach. Whether he is usin paint-ball tag to illustrate a point at Sunday services, riding a Harley-Davidson through the sanctuary, o broadcasting his message on television Treat is passionate about making sure his message about renewing the mind is heard.

"By confronting the truth and embracing God's life, rather than conforming to what is wrong with the world, Christians can achieve a meaningful life with a vision and purpose," Treat says. "Abundant lif is about always moving forward an rising higher. The abundant life of God is a life that grows and moves forward every day."

To succeed, Treat provides peop with a practical map leading to God's way of living that has inspired thou sands of people from all walks of lif and backgrounds to join Christian Faith Center. He encourages peopl to follow what he calls the five Rs: be responsible, rethink what you believe, reject the old way, review the new, and resound.

Whether using paint-ball tag to illustrate a point at Sunday services, riding a Harley-Davidson through the sanctuary, or broadcasting his message on television, Treat is passionate about making sure his message is heard.

ard Path to Follow

n stage, Treat carries an energetic warmth and dynamic presence. though he has captivated many ople throughout the Pacific North- st and abroad, he wasn't always certain of his destiny.

Following a teenage bout with ugs, which resulted in several arrests, eat chose to serve 21 months in drug abilitation rather than in jail. It was the Christian-based rehab center at he discovered his calling. He ved as the center's assistant director ile completing his bachelor's degree theology at Seattle Bible School. eat was attending Bible school when met his wife, Wendy, whose fam- includes generations of pastors.

In 1980, the duo started Christian ith Center in the foyer of a Christian hool with a congregation of 30. To- y, Christian Faith Center has built astonishing ministry designed to ow strong families through its schools d to reinvent ways to build faith. he ministry employs more than 100 ople, and utilizes a large number volunteers to provide an assortment services, including valet parking, presso stands, and special events men, women, and children.

Christian Faith Center hosts tradi- nal community celebrations at hristmas and Easter, as well as more novative activities such as an indoor dependence Day Harley-Davidson rade. The church is geared toward odern-day lifestyles and helping people find God in everything they do.

CFC's Next Level Youth Church (NXL) engages teens to conduct weekly, teen-oriented services with creative music and an impressive sound stage. NXL also includes a special Saturday night Youth Center hangout with music, pool tables, air hockey, a snack bar, and video games.

"When we really know God's Word—the Bible—our lives show it in every way," says Treat. "Our marriages, children, careers, finances, and futures will be blessed as we walk with Him."

Captivating programs, activities, and education for children and youth are a priority at Christian Faith Center, which include Christian Faith Schools and Dominion College (top).

Next Level Youth Church provides teens with activities and "out of the box" programs at a special youth center hangout (left).

Christian Faith Center provides weekly church services to more than 6,000 residents in the Seattle area and reaches an international audience through *Living on Course*, a weekday television show (right).

Headquartered in downtown Seatti near historic Pioneer Square, Pinnacle Realty Management Company is an i ternational real estate investment management firm that provides both mult family residential and commercial real estate owners and investors with a broa scope of realty services, including the acquisition, disposition, rehabilitatio property management, financing, and repositioning of real estate asse

throughout the nation. With a total portfolio value of more than $4.6 billion, Pinnacle's commercial holdings include office, retail, and industrial properties in 41 states and 264 cities in the United States and Canada, placing the firm among the top commercial management companies in the country. In addition to property management, Pinnacle also provides facilities management and leasing services.

"The guiding principle is really quite simple," says Stan Harrelson, president and CEO. "We're a service organization. Service has been and will always be our top priority." Pinnacle clients range from North America to Asia, Europe, and the Caribbean. The company serves more than 250 institutions, pension funds, private partnerships, foreign investors, sole owners, and government housing groups.

Steady Growth

Pinnacle was founded in 1980 by John Goodman, the current chairman. Its original name was Goodman Management Group, and it specialized in multifamily residential management. As the company established a national identity, Goodman focused his expertise on expanding the firm's national management and brokerage networks, as well as developing international client and investor relationships.

Harrelson became a partner in 1985, and the firm was renamed Goodman Financial Services (GFS). A steady period of nationwide expansion followed, and in 1994, the company acquired Houston's Sovereign National Management Company. The operations were merged into Pinnacle Realty Management Company, which now boasts more than 2,800 employees; four regional offic in Seattle, Sacramento, Dallas, and Orlando; and 35 branch offices.

Harrelson directs Pinnacle's strategic planning efforts toward long-term growth and profitability He also guides the development of the company's vision and corporat culture. In keeping with his belief in customer service, Harrelson is committed to a constant alignmen of corporate goals and client needs and he works closely with senior staf to provide continuous reinforcemen of the firm's goals.

Pinnacle's local identity is personifie in Ward McLain, president of the company's Northwest region, whic

Pinnacle Realty Management Company's international headquarters is located in the historic Pioneer Square district in downtown Seattle (right).

Stan Harrelson, Pinnacle president and chief executive officer often finds similarities between being a successful athlete and being a leader of the largest third-party manager of multifamily real estate in the United States (left).

STEWART HOPKINS PHOTOGRAPHY

cludes Washington, Oregon, Idaho, Montana, Alaska, British Columbia, and Saskatchewan. Within that vast range, McLain is responsible for the operations and business growth for multifamily, commercial, brokerage, and public housing activities.

Definitive Expertise

Customer service is the guiding principle at Pinnacle, but the company also touts its entrepreneurial roots and its commitment to talented employees, along with solid market knowledge on the local and national fronts.

Employees earn one-and-a-half times as much as their competitors in the field, according to Harrelson, who says, "Our assets ride the elevators." When employees do leave the firm, it's usually to form their own companies rather than to go to work for a rival.

It's not uncommon for Pinnacle to recruit talent from outside the real estate industry. Harrelson believes in hiring attitude and training for skill. Some of Pinnacle's leasing agents come from retailers such as Nordstrom and the Bon Marche, where a service-oriented attitude is prevalent.

By combining a national and local presence, Pinnacle has established a yardstick by which other real estate management companies will be measured. Prospective clients are attracted to a company that can demonstrate expertise on a small scale while sporting a geographic range that literally runs from coast to coast.

The knowledge Pinnacle has gained over the years is an asset the company refuses to hide. That allows Harrelson to look clients in the eye and speak with authority. Pinnacle has reached the point where its reputation is enough of an asset to bring clients calling, looking for an expert opinion. They usually get it, and Harrelson isn't afraid to explain hard realities to customers.

"We are not apologetic at all about what we know to be true," says Harrelson. "We are applying a solution to get the customers what they want, and doing it right."

One of Pinnacle's surprising attributes—an aspect that separates it from many other property management firms—is that the firm doesn't own the properties it manages. By eliminating the ownership aspect, Pinnacle is able to focus exclusively on the management side and cater to client needs more effectively, while avoiding some of the common pitfalls associated with ownership.

STEWART HOPKINS PHOTOGRAPHY

John Goodman, Pinnacle chairman and founder

The company's steady growth has allowed it to build a strong national infrastructure, making it easier to respond to client needs quickly, as well as effectively managing portfolios for clients with assets in multiple states.

Pinnacle's management professionals create value through day-to-day supervision and long-term strategic planning. They analyze market trends to determine how to effectively position a property within a given market, then evaluate property operations and develop a customized marketing, leasing, and management strategy to maximize its potential value.

Services: A Multifamily Foundation

Third-party management of multifamily real estate is Pinnacle's trademark, and the company is a recognized national leader. Apartments, public housing, military housing, and even college dormitories figure into the mix. Unit size is diverse, ranging from an eight-unit building in Seattle to a 1,149-unit complex in Jacksonville, Florida.

The ownership clientele spans a wide range. Pinnacle's institutional partners include insurance companies, trust funds, Wall Street firms, foreign investors, wealthy individuals, and limited partnerships.

Ward McLain, president of Pinnacle's Northwest region

Pinnacle's list of specific services includes asset renovation, development advisory services, asset repositioning, and lease-up campaign expertise, as well as networked computer systems, training, risk management, customized marketing, and responsive resident/tenant retention programs.

Multifamily management involves more than picking up the rent and pruning the shrubs. Pinnacle's aggressive service commitment is driven by the nature of a business where contracts can be canceled on a month's notice. Tenant services such as insurance and newspaper subscriptions are examples of the value-added approach Pinnacle likes to promote.

The attraction of residential property management is relatively simple: rent revenue grows more quickly on the

STEWART HOPKINS

Clockwise from top left:
Pinnacle professionals analyze market trends to determine how to effectively position a property within a given market.

One of Pinnacle's surprising attributes is that it does not own any of the properties it manages, which allows the company to concentrate on showcasing its managed properties and meeting the needs of the client more effectively.

Pinnacle combines its management services with a brokerage division that has clientele from nearly a dozen countries.

residential side. Shorter-term leases give nimble companies the opportunity to move in and out of properties and to adjust more readily to the rhythms of the market.

Success comes from the willingness to take risks, and Pinnacle has shown its creativity in several settings. In 1997, the company took charge of a 25-year-old Florida apartment complex with so much water damage the city of Orlando had condemned it. Following a $3.8 million renovation, the site soared to 95 percent occupancy, and subsequently sold for $15.6 million—$9 million more than the purchase price 18 months earlier.

A similar success story emerged in Pinnacle's backyard when the company was selected to manage Whispering Pines, a 246-unit public housing community in Snohomish County with a history of crime and neglect. Following a massive renovation effort, the crime rate dropped drastically and residents began to take pride in their surroundings.

Continued diversification spurred Pinnacle's entry into the affordable housing market in 1994. By employing new approaches to repositioning public housing, the company has built a reputation for transforming troubled properties into desirable communities.

The government trend toward privatization of public housing has played to Pinnacle's strengths. With approximately 1.6 million public housing units nationwide, the niche is a big one. A measure signed in 1996 by President Bill Clinton authorized privatization of all family housing on U.S. military installations, flooding the market with 385,000 new units.

Pinnacle has seized the opportunity, and now ranks as the largest private manager of public housing in the country. Currently, it has more than 16,480 units of affordable housing under management, including approximately 6,424 public housing units and 10,060 Section 42 Low Income Housing Tax Credit units. Locally, its portfolio includes consulting contracts in Seattle, King, and Snohomish counties. Portland, Oregon; Chicago; Atlanta; Miami; and Puerto Rico are among the other contract areas.

A Potent Combination

Pinnacle combines its management services with an investment brokerage division to create an efficient one-two punch for clients. The brokerage side completed commercial and multifamily investment real estate transactions totaling nearly $800 million in 1998 and $650 million in 1999. In that same time, Pinnacle has brokered in excess of 10,000 multifamily apartment units. In addition, the company has handled the sale of nearly 5 million square feet of commercial assets.

As a market leader in third-party fee management, Pinnacle is able to create value for buyers and sellers by working with on-site staff and in-house property management experts in a given market. This gives the team of brokers, who average 15 years of real estate experience apiece e ability to deliver more accurate sight into a prospective building's ture performance opportunities.

Pinnacle currently has a team of) brokers in 14 major U.S. cities d 10 states—combining multimily, office, industrial, and retail perience. In fact, Pinnacle broers are becoming a nationally own commodity, while retaining e local experience that is critical r selling individual assets. The mpany's management expertise s developed a market niche that ients want, creating value for oth buyers and sellers.

Vast experience on the manageent side gives Pinnacle brokers a luable edge in terms of product owledge, as well as relationships ith a large pool of buyers and sells. The company works to build lid partnerships with these and her clients, enabling it to underand a client's specific needs when it comes to buying and selling assets.

Without the leverage of ownership, Pinnacle has to outwork its competitors to win and retain business. Responsive client service is the foundation that enables the company to deliver market-leading asset performance. To stay ahead, Pinnacle offers a smorgasbord of value-added services to enhance the firm's property management and brokerage divisions. These services include construction management, risk management, accounting, information technology, human resources, and training.

Pinnacle's market position allows it to be selective in its client relationships. Harrelson's belief in "good clients" translates to partnerships that allow the company to feel comfortable, and it's an approach that's likely to continue.

"Fun is right up there with profit from our standpoint," says Harrelson. "We liked how we felt when we were a small company. We're selective in the use of our time. I'd rather have less business of better quality than to be big for the sake of it."

With such a priority on fun, it is no surprise that the company's headquarters is near the soon-to-be-constructed, new home of Paul Allen's Seattle Seahawks. An eye-popping display of sports memorabilia graces Pinnacle's lobby. Helmets, baseballs, gloves, jerseys—most are autographed, and the names are downright intimidating: Ken Griffey Jr., Gary Payton, and John Elway, to name only a few. If it isn't already clear, Harrelson plays with the big boys.

Harrelson dismisses the impressive collection when asked. "It's just my thing," he says. Still, it's hard not to see a certain spiritual similarity between the athletes and a leader of the largest third-party manager of multifamily real estate in the United States.

▲ STEWART HOPKINS PHOTOGRAPHY

Pinnacle diversified in the 1990s to become a dominant player in commercial management and leasing (left).

Members of the Northwest region property management staff perform on-site inspections, an important part of Pinnacle's customer service (right).

ATTACHMATE CORPORATION, LOCATED O BELLEVUE'S I-90 CORRIDOR, IS THE WORLD'S LARGEST PRIVATELY HELD PC SOFTWAR COMPANY. FOR MORE THAN 18 YEARS, ATTACHMATE HAS BEEN A LEADING SUPPLIER C ENTERPRISE INFORMATION ACCESS AND APPLICATION INTEGRATION SOLUTIONS, SERVIN MAJOR CORPORATIONS AND GOVERNMENT AGENCIES WORLDWIDE. ● ATTACHMATE WA NAMED 1999'S BEST LARGE COMPANY TO WORK FOR IN WASHINGTON B

Washington CEO magazine, and it boasts an employee-oriented environment. Offering such amenities as an annual holiday gala and summer picnic, as well as weekly unwinders for all employees to socialize, Attachmate proudly wears its reputation as a people-friendly workplace.

Attachmate's e-Vantage™ products provide client access to host systems such as mainframes, AS/400®, VAX®, and UNIX®. Simply put, The company's specialty is helping disparate types of computers communicate with each other. Attachmate specializes in Web-to-enterprise and desktop-to-host business solutions, as well as management software. The company also provides expert consulting services and boasts an award-winning technical support organization. More than 80 percent of Fortune 500 and Global 2000 corporations rely on Attachmate products for connecting to and leveraging their enterprise information residing on legacy systems.

FOUNDED IN 1982 BY CEO FRANK PRITT, ATTACHMATE CORPORATION EMPLOYS MORE THAN 1,500 PEOPLE WORLDWIDE, WITH OFFICES IN 50 NORTH AMERICAN CITIES AND 30 COUNTRIES.

Stability in Endurance

Unlike many high-tech companies, Attachmate has a history that reaches back farther than a few months. Founded in 1982 by CEO Frank Pritt, the company employs more than 1,500 people worldwide, with offices in 50 North American cities and 30 countries. The company's leaders respond to the opportunities and challenges that customers face with new ways to capitalize on innovation while leveraging existing technology.

The latest challenge for Attachmate is the growing world of e-commerce. The company was specializing in software long before the Internet took off in the 1990s, but the firm still found it necessary to adjust to the new shape of the market. The world of on-line retail is booming—holiday Internet spending reached $4 billion in 1999, compared to $650 million in 1997, according to Internet commerce experts at Forrester Research.

In response to this industry change, Attachmate shifted its focus, reconfiguring its sales and marketing departments and redefining its vision. The company has also developed its e-Vantage line of products, designed to help businesses manage e-commerce more effectively.

Stories of Attachmate's successful ventures abound. Credit Suisse used Attachmate software to improve service to its clients, while upgrading internal systems to make them faster, more intuitive, and easier to use. Th Bosch Company established an on-lir ordering system using e-Vantage, giv ing dealers a more convenient metho of placing orders and sharpening Bosch's competitive edge.

Other Attachmate e-Vantage customers include Pennsylvania's Allegheny County, Brazil's largest tele phone company, and Sharp Products Attachmate products helped South Australia's vehicle registration and licensing agency streamline its services to motorists as well.

The Potential of Partnership

Recognizing the complicated cha lenges of maintaining internal computer networks while providin greater access to outside Web traffic i the course of establishing an on-lin business presence, Attachmate embarked on collaborative partnership with two companies in spring 200C

Attachmate's partnership with Siebel Systems, provider of e-busines applications software, brings togethe two companies with expertise in man aging business information. Packetee another ally, is a leading provider o Internet infrastructure systems. Together, these companies will provid compatible tools to assist customers in the continuing development of their e-businesses.

The partnerships continue a collaborative tradition that has long bee part of Attachmate's overall approach Attachmate also has a long-standin strategic business partnership with the Unisys Corporation, and is the premier provider of desktop connec tivity for the Unisys community.

Employee Advantages

In July 1999, *Washington CEO* magazine tapped Attachmate as th best large company to work for in Washington, reflecting the company' corporate commitment to recruitin and retaining quality employees. A

ide range of employee-friendly ben-
'its has contributed to the firm's
putation.

Technical training, certification
rograms, and tuition reimbursement
e available to Attachmate employees.
chievements are recognized and
warded with individual cash awards,
orting event tickets, and generous
mpany bonuses.

In addition to standard benefits
ch as 401(k) plans and medical/den-
l insurance, the company offers on-
e fitness facilities, massages, financial
minars, and parenting classes. In
ntrast to the image of most software
mpanies, Attachmate encourages
s employees to live a balanced life
d pursue interests outside the office.

Along with holiday parties and
mily-oriented picnics, the company
bsidizes attendance at various cul-
ral events. After-work sports and
eekly social events preserve a small-
mpany feel, something that remains
nportant to Pritt. The firm's CEO
a regular in the dunk tank at com-
any picnics, and he is known as a
ractical joker.

Community Participation

Community involvement is another key aspect of the Attachmate philosophy. The company's ties to local organizations cover a wide range of charitable groups. Among them are the Eastside Literacy Council, a nonprofit group that trains volunteers to tutor adults who are having difficulty reading or writing at the level they need to thrive; New Beginnings, an organization that assists women and children fleeing from domestic violence; Childhaven, a nonprofit corporation dedicated to providing programs aimed at eliminating child abuse and neglect; the Harborview Burn Center, a project that uses virtual reality technologies to ease the pain and suffering of burn patients; the Boys and Girls Club; and the Nature Conservancy.

With successful practices in place, collaboration among high-tech leaders, and a healthy work ethic among employees, Attachmate Corporation has created its own brand of success in the ever changing technology industry.

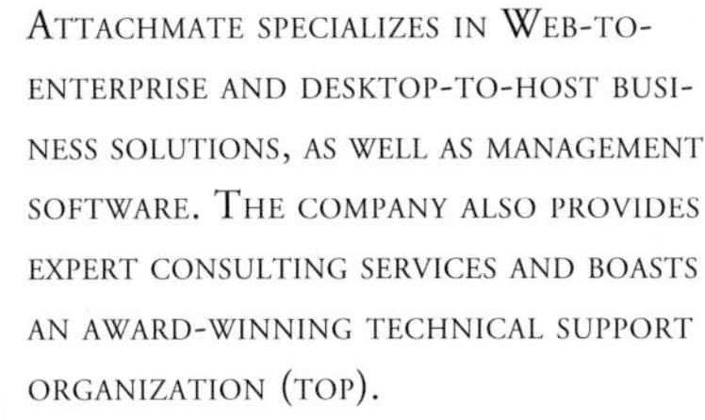

Attachmate specializes in Web-to-enterprise and desktop-to-host business solutions, as well as management software. The company also provides expert consulting services and boasts an award-winning technical support organization (top).

Attachmate's e-Vantage™ products provide client access to host systems such as mainframes, AS/400®, VAX®, and UNIX®. Simply put, Attachmate's specialty is helping disparate types of computers communicate with each other.

For Fran Bigelow, chocolate is trul a matter of taste. She got into the confectionery business because of "th desire to make a difference in chocolate," she says. "I have a passion for chocolat I want to make taste the paramount thing. It shouldn't disappoint you whe you put it in your mouth. It should always taste better than it looks." ● Chocolat lovers are not the only ones who appreciate Bigelow's pursuit of the perfec confection: food industry critics laud her efforts as well. Corby Kummer, senior editor and food writer for the *Atlantic Monthly* and a coauthor of The Book of Chocolate, describes Bigelow as "the country's best all-around chocolate maker."

Bigelow's dedication to excellence has kept her company small and her level of quality high. Fran's Chocolates produces handmade, hand-wrapped, premium chocolate for the high-end gourmet customer, based on her own original recipes. Creations such as Fran's Gold Bars have earned extravagant praise from food critics around the world.

The Ingredients for Success

When Bigelow founded Fran's Chocolates in 1982, the company was a two-employee operation in a Seattle storefront. She had spent the 1970s raising her two children, after graduating from the University of Washington with a degree in business.

Along the way, Bigelow's interest in cooking increased, drawing inspiration from Julia Child. Eventually, she studied cooking under Josephine Araldo, a 1921 graduate of Le Cordon Bleu cooking school in Paris. Bigelow then enrolled in California Culinary Academy and worked as a dessert chef in two restaurants. Her quest for better chocolate recipes and better tastes had begun. "I was neve a big caramel fan," Bigelow says. "Then I figured out that I'd never really had exceptional caramel."

In the early days, the shop wasn't focused solely on chocolate. Bigelow concentrated on selling specialty cakes to area restaurants. Originally, the shop had two small tables where guests could sit down to enjoy slices of dessert.

Gradually, word of the woman making European-style chocolates got around, and demand for Bigelow' products grew. The shop on Madison Street could no longer accommodat her business expansion. Bigelow established her Laboratoire du Chocolat on East Pike Street, and opened a second retail store in Bellevue in 1996. Fran's Chocolates now includes a thriving mail-order business; online orders at the company Web site, www.franschocolates.com; and

Fran Bigelow's dedication to excellence has kept her company small and her level of quality high. Fran's Chocolates produces handmade, hand-wrapped, premium chocolate for the high-end gourmet customer, based on her own original recipes.

With a taste for quality and an eye for the aesthetic, Bigelow maintains the unique approach that has prompted her—and Fran's Chocolates—success.

istribution at Williams-Sonoma tores throughout the nation.

lending Creativity and Chemistry

Success hasn't spoiled Bigelow's firm commitment to quality. he continues to produce chocolate n small batches, with no additives r preservatives. Bigelow does not terally manufacture chocolate her-elf—no bean roasting or processing akes place at the Laboratoire du Chocolat. Instead, she combines the lavors of the world's best chocolate n her own recipes.

"What I do is blend for taste," Bigelow says. "It's personal, and it's what passes our standard for what will make an exceptional product. 'm looking to give the customer aste—a product that's quite distinc-ive to us." Bigelow's taste draws on European tradition. For example, she loesn't like high sugar levels that ob-cure the flavor. And when it comes o truffles, according to Bigelow, here should be a slight snap as he outer surface breaks, a sign of freshness.

"I love the chemistry of it," Bigelow says. "I love recipe research. love testing things until we find he specific ingredient or technique hat's going to make it."

Among nearly 100 creations, rang-ng from delicate truffles to raspberry sauce to chocolate creams, Fran's Gold Bar is the company's signature item. The company sells almost 500,000 a year. Gold Bars start out as a pool of warm caramel, spread across a shallow metal tray. A liberal load of almonds or macadamia nuts is added, and the mixture is then allowed to set. After being sliced into individual sections, the nutty caramel is dipped in an outer layer of Belgian chocolate, and each bar is wrapped in gold foil.

Savoring the Acclaim

The food world loves Bigelow. Her creations are consistent final-ists in national confectioner's com-petitions, and critics sing her praises. *The Chicago Tribune* wrote a glowing review saying, "You could be in a jewelry shop. The cakes on display are exquisite, the candies are hand-dipped jewels. One soon discovers they taste as good as they look."

Fran's Chocolates continues to create new products to please the palate. The company's new Park Bar, a soft caramel studded with roasted Virginia peanuts and covered with premium milk chocolate, was a finalist in the outstanding confec-tion category at the 1999 Summer Fancy Food Show in New York. Bigelow's ice-cream recipes, featur-ing flavors such as Ginger Lime,

Turbinado Burnt Sugar Caramel, and Chocolate au Chocolat, are top sellers.

But Bigelow is not likely to open a factory. Mass production is not her style. "The thing that holds us back, but propels us at the same time, is doing these recipes the same way," she says. With a taste for quality and an eye for the aesthetic, Bigelow maintains the unique approach that has prompted her—and Fran's Chocolates—success.

Bigelow's creations are consistent finalists in national confectioner's competitions, and critics sing her praises. The *Chicago Tribune* wrote a glowing review saying, "You could be in a jewelry shop. The cakes on display are exquisite, the candies are hand-dipped jewels. One soon discovers they taste as good as they look."

IT INSPIRES RAVE REVIEWS FROM PEOPLE OF AL AGES, EVEN THOUGH ITS MEMBERS PAY A FEE FOR THE PRIVILEGE OF SHOPPING THERE. IT HA BEEN HOST TO COUNTLESS ANNIVERSARIES AND CELEBRATIONS. IT IS SO MUCH OF A CULTURA ICON IT'S BEEN THE SUBJECT OF A *Seinfeld* SITCOM EPISODE AND WAS VOTED ONE OF TH TOP FIVE CHEAP DINNER DATES BY JAY LENO. IT'S COSTCO WHOLESALE. AND IT ALL STARTE IN SEATTLE IN 1983. FROM ITS CORPORATE HEADQUARTERS IN ISSAQUAH, AMONG TH shadows of the looming Cascade Range, Costco Wholesale operates 331 warehouses worldwide—238 in the United States, 59 in Canada, nine in the United Kingdom, three in South Korea, three in Taiwan, and one in Japan, as well as 18 in Mexico with a joint-venture partner. The number of Costco cardholders today exceeds 30 million, and the company employs more than 75,000 people worldwide.

Something for Everyone

Costco's members are fiercely loyal, vowing to whoever will listen that they will never again buy toilet paper or televisions or tires anywhere else. Each and every member has his or her own Costco story. Of course, it's not hard for Costco to have something for everyone when the typical warehouse averages 135,000 square feet. Members select their products from pallets, a departure from the classic retail tradition of meticulously arranged floor displays and carefully ordered product placement.

From computers to croissants, Norelco to Nabisco, Costco offers thousands of items for its members to choose from for their homes, offices, or businesses. The result is a shopping experience members often refer to as both "exciting" and a "treasure hunt atmosphere."

Since 1983, when the first warehouse opened near the now-departed Kingdome, Costco has focused on providing top customer service and member satisfaction. Since its inception, Costco's cardinal rules have remained intact: to bring the highest-quality goods and services to its members at the best possible prices; to sell only those items that provide a savings to its members; and to unconditionally guarantee not only its products and services, but also the Costco membership itself.

Costco must be doing something right. Since that first warehouse opened, the company has grown to become the seventh-largest retailer in the United States, selling more than $30 billion in goods and services annually.

"I have never added up exactly how much I spend at Costco, but I'm there all the time," says membe Cynthia Stang. "I greatly appreciat the savings."

A Unique Warehousing Concept

Costco warehouses carry quality, brand-name merchandise at sub stantially lower prices than those typically found at more conventiona retailers. The company combines immense buying power with low overhead costs to create a formidable retai presence. The company's increasing levels of buying power allow Costc to acquire goods at a lower price

COSTCO WHOLESALE WAREHOUSES CARRY QUALITY, BRAND-NAME MERCHANDISE AT SUBSTANTIALLY LOWER PRICES THAN THOSE TYPICALLY FOUND AT MORE CONVENTIONAL RETAILERS. THE COMPANY COMBINES IMMENSE BUYING POWER WITH LOW OVERHEAD COSTS TO CREATE A FORMIDABLE RETAIL PRESENCE.

COSTCO HAS WAREHOUSES THROUGHOUT THE UNITED STATES, AND IN CANADA, THE UNITED KINGDOM, SOUTH KOREA, TAIWAN, JAPAN, AND MEXICO. ITS WAREHOUSES AVERAGE 135,000 SQUARE FEET.

FROM COMPUTERS TO CROISSANTS, NORELCO TO NABISCO, COSTCO OFFERS THOUSANDS OF ITEMS FOR ITS MEMBERS TO CHOOSE FROM FOR THEIR HOMES, OFFICES, OR BUSINESSES.

an before. The rule is simple: Take e majority of any such savings and ass it on to the members in the form even lower prices than before. It's idea Costco's founders created the late 1970s. The concept has awned a $60 billion industry, fueled y annual sales growth of 15 percent nce 1987.

"Costco offers lower prices and etter values by eliminating virtually l the frills and costs historically associated with wholesalers and retailers, cluding salespeople, fancy buildings nd features, delivery, billing, and counts receivable," says Jim Sinegal, resident and CEO. "We run a tight peration with extremely low overhead, which enables us to reflect dramatic pricing to our members. Saving our members money on the purchase of goods and services is what Costco is all about."

At any given minute, Costco warehouses contain a cross section of society. A young mother stocks up on disposable diapers. Founding partners of a new start-up business choose new office furniture. A convenience store owner replenishes his supply of candy, gum, and snack food. Teens peruse the CDs and videos, while restaurant chefs select produce for the meals they will be preparing later that evening.

Members often stop at the Food Court for a slice of freshly baked pizza and a soda, or for a Costco hot dog that would do any stadium proud. Forty million of these famous Costco hot dogs are sold each year.

EACH YEAR, JOHN AND SHARON LISICICH CELEBRATE THEIR WEDDING ANNIVERSARY AT THEIR FAVORITE DINING ESTABLISHMENT—COSTCO'S FOOD COURT.

The Legendary Hot Dog

Already an avidly loyal group, Costco members' enthusiasm goes off the chart when the subject of hot dogs comes up. The hot dogs at Costco's Food Court are a universal favorite. Many appreciate the $1.50 sticker price for a hot dog and refillable soda, which makes it possible to take the family out to dinner more often than ever before. Members even go so far as to write fan mail to Costco, relating their stories—many of which get reprinted in *The Costco Connection* and *Costco Wholesale Today.*

"My son and I have a date every two weeks at Costco—just the two of us—for two Polish hot dogs and a soda pop," writes a single mom. "It is a highlight for him and has become a family tradition for us."

Even on those special occasions when money is no object, the Costco hot dog tops a lot of lists. One member, Miriam Starr, reportedly passed up a lunch reservation at the world-famous Spago's in Los Angeles to celebrate her 90th birthday at the Costco in Van Nuys. For the fifth consecutive year, her birthday meal of choice: the Costco hot dog. Another member, Dorothy Thomas from Prescott, Arizona, writes, "We eat at Costco at least five nights a week. We love the pizza, hot dogs, and [frozen] yogurt."

Nationally known brands are staples on Costco's ample shelves, but the company also offers its own Kirkland signature line of products, designed as a value-priced, top-quality alternative for cost-conscious consumers.

When Al and CeCe Schubert—longtime Costco members from Palm Desert—stopped by the Coachella Valley warehouse to grab a hot dog and soft drink, they found 34 of Al's closest friends on hand to celebrate his 65th birthday. "We've been going to Costco for years," says Al. "My friend Ed and I always say you can't go to Costco without buying a hot dog, but this was quite a shocker."

And then there is the story of Sharon and John Lisicich. Each year, they celebrate their wedding anniversary by visiting Costco. "Costco is such a special part of our anniversary," says Sharon. "We shop at Costco about once a week. The staff is wonderful, and the customer service and products are terrific." On that special night, it's just Sharon and John, with a couple of all-beef hot dogs with mustard in hand, gazing at the sun as it sets over 300 or 400 cars in the parking lot.

The Spectrum of Products and Services

It takes more than a great hot dog to keep several hundred cars in every Costco parking lot. Costco prides itself on its extensive selection of products, which include groceries, candy, appliances, television and sound equipment, electronics, automotive supplies, tires, toys, hardware, sporting goods, fine jewelry, watches, cameras, books, housewares, apparel, health and beauty aids, tobacco, furniture, and office supplies and equipment.

Nationally known brands are staples on Costco's ample shelves, but the company also offers its own Kirkland signature line of product designed as a value-priced, top-qualit alternative for cost-conscious consumers. Kirkland products includ diapers, apparel, film, luggage, appliances, batteries, tires, cookies, coffee, health and beauty aids, detergent, and more.

Among the items most popula with Costco members are the bakery products that are made on the premises. Costco's in-house baker products include cakes, pies, croissants, cookies, pastries, breads, an its legendary, huge muffins. In 200 alone, Costco sold nearly 250 millio croissants and muffins.

"Members can watch us bake the items," says Sue McConnaha, Costco's vice president of bakery operations. "That's unique for retai bakeries. We enjoy talking with th

Costco offers such services as self-service gasoline stations, printing centers, pharmacies, 1 hour photo labs, optical departments, and hearing-aid centers.

embers while we create the perfect .ke for their special occasion, or st the right pie for their dessert. 's a lot of fun, and there's nothing ‹e the smell of fresh-baked goods afting through the warehouse."

It's this old-fashioned approach at has helped make Costco one of e nation's most successful self- rvice, seven-day-a-week bakeries. luch like the famous Costco hot ›g, bakery items have become syn- ıymous with the Costco concept, cluding the convenient, custom- :corated half-sheet cakes that fit any :casion; all-butter croissants that e a hit at any breakfast; chocolate ıunk cookies; and a variety of gi- ıntic muffins, to name just a few.

In recent years, the company has lded further to its spectrum of rvices. Deli items, prepared entrées, ıd fresh produce and meats help ·ing members back to the ware- ›use frequently. Self-service gaso- ıe stations have become prominent atures at many U.S. locations, and s not uncommon for lines to form the gas pumps as word of the excel- ıt pricing spreads. Costco also offers ch goods and services as pharmacy, ›tical, one-hour photo, hearing ds, and printing.

The E-commerce trend hasn't escaped the company's notice. Costco first entered the world of the Internet in 1995 with an informational Web site. Since November 1998, members have been able to purchase merchandise and services on-line at www.costco.com. Computers, electronics, flowers, and major appliances—even diamond rings—can be purchased on the site and delivered anywhere in the continental United States.

Creating a Sense of Community

There are less tangible but equally powerful elements of belonging to the Costco community of members. Costco's presence in the neighborhoods where it locates warehouses is felt in many ways. Employees typically are involved in fund-raising for local causes, often with matching funds provided by the company. Costco and its employees donated more than $10 million to charitable causes in 1999.

Contributions to communities don't always come in the form of dollars. Everyday actions by Costco and its employees impact the lives of community members. There are the Costco employees who volunteer time each week to tutor young students at neighborhood schools. There's the Costco warehouse manager who instructed employees to distribute cookies to drivers stuck in a traffic jam near his warehouse. And there is the company's ability to bring in extra supplies of generators and drinking water to help communities survive natural disasters like hurricanes, floods, or tornadoes.

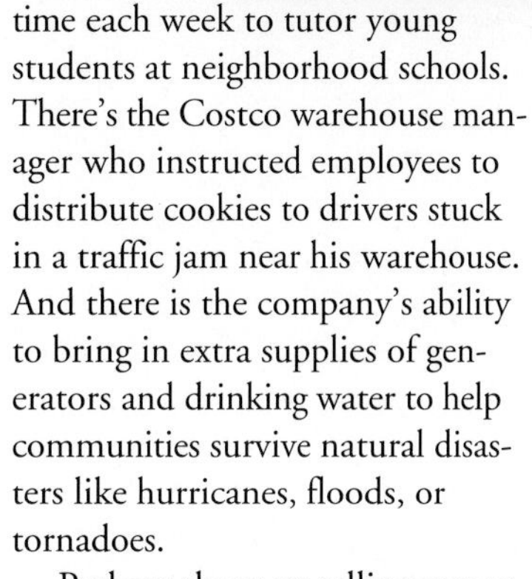

Perhaps the most telling way to illustrate Costco members' love affair with the Costco warehouse is the simple fact that people visit Costco even when they're on vacation. Susan and Robert Stanton of Seattle took time out on their trip to Japan to stop by the first Costco warehouse in Fukuoka. "It was great fun," the Stantons say. "We saw a teenage girl carrying a Costco pizza box and we smiled in the recognition that some things are universal. It was comforting to find a slice of Americana."

With reactions like that, it's not surprising that Costco's leaders foresee continued expansion of the membership base in the coming years. Through ongoing innovation and additional services, Costco Wholesale will continue to lead in the market it helped define.

Costco members, who pay a fee to shop, refer to their warehouse visits as both "exciting" and a "treasure hunt atmosphere."

Costco's 331 warehouses offer something for everyone, including groceries, appliances, electronics, fine jewelry, apparel, office supplies, and furniture, all at low warehouse prices.

1986-2001

1986 AT&T Wireless Services
1988 Boullioun Aviation Services, Inc.
1989 Washington CEO Magazine
1990 Wizards of the Coast
1992 The City Church
1992 Seattle Theatre Group
1993 Covenant Celebration Church
1994 RealNetworks, Inc.
1994 Western Wireless Corporation/
VoiceStream Wireless Corporation
1994 Wade Cook Financial Corporation
1995 PacifiCare of Washington
1995 Insignia International Inc.
1996 Expedia, Inc.
1996 NikeTown
1996 Seattle Homes and Lifestyles
1997 Activate Corporation
1997 Freddie's Club Casino
1999 W Hotel

SINCE 1986, AT&T WIRELESS SERVICE HAS BEEN A SHINING EXAMPLE OF A COMPANY WORKING BOTH WITH AND FOR TH COMMUNITY IT SERVES. BASED IN REDMOND, AT&T WIRELESS OPERATES ONE OF TH LARGEST DIGITAL WIRELESS NETWORKS IN NORTH AMERICA, WITH MORE THAN 14 MILLIO SUBSCRIBERS RECEIVING WIRELESS VOICE AND DATA COMMUNICATION SERVICES. TH COMPANY, A WHOLLY OWNED SUBSIDIARY OF AT&T CORPORATION, IS THE PRODUC of a 1994 merger between McCaw Cellular Communications of Kirkland and AT&T—at the time, the fifth-largest merger in U.S. business history.

AT&T Wireless recently established its own presence on the New York Stock Exchange with an initial public offering. With more than 21,000 employees worldwide—2,500 of whom live and work in Seattle—the company continues to ride the wireless wave, launching products and expanding into new markets on a regular basis. At its Redmond campus, the company occupies six buildings with satellite offices across the region, from Bellingham to Vancouver to Spokane.

"Making our busy lives much simpler and more manageable" is the company credo, according to Ken Woo, spokesman for AT&T Wireless. Handheld wireless computers with Internet access and E-mailing capability, along with palm-sized videoconferencing device are some of the innovations the com pany anticipates in the near future.

Emergency communication is one of the fundamental needs addressed by wireless services, and AT&T Wireless recognizes the importance of providing it. A longtim partnership with the American Red Cross allows AT&T Wireless to provide services to the relief agency and help it develop a nationwide communications network.

JERRY GAY

AT&T WIRELESS SERVICES' FAMILY FOURTH OF JULY CELEBRATION ON SEATTLE'S LAKE UNION DRAWS TENS OF THOUSANDS OF PEOPLE TO WATCH THE WORK OF JAPANESE FIREWORKS MASTER SEIJI KASE.

A Priority on Community

"We feel strongly about community involvement," says Woo. "It's really our number one priority Advancing technology is number two."

The company participates in a variety of local activities, searching for partnership opportunities that allow employees to work with community groups and nonprofit organizations. The focus is on empowering communities by giving them the resources they need to improve health and human services, promote diversity, protect the environment, and stimulate volunteerism.

Local event sponsorships includ the annual Jingle Bell Run for Arthritis and the Northwest AIDS Walk. Examples of internally based community involvement efforts include the AT&T Cares program, which connects employees to nonprofit organizations in their communities. The company provides grants to local organizations, coupled with employee time. For one day each year, participants in the AT&T Cares program are granted a paid leave day for volunteer work at the organization of their choice.

Another recent endeavor is the AT&T Safe Schools program. Recognizing the need for security on school campuses, and observing the

AT&T Wireless encourages employees to volunteer for community work through such as programs AT&T Cares and AT&T Safe Schools.

metimes fragmented or antiquated ▸ JEFF BRAVERMAN
mmunications systems on school
ounds, the company has begun to
ovide grants for cellular phones to
hool safety officials. The phones
n be used in emergency situations,
to make regular communication
ore streamlined and efficient. "We
scovered there was a great need
r this kind of communication
n school properties," says Woo.

ntributions to Culture

Promoting cultural events is another area of emphasis for the mpany, which regularly sponsors oductions at Seattle's A Contemorary Theatre. The AT&T Summer ights at the Pier concert series on lliott Bay has become a much anicipated annual event that enjoys itical acclaim. The setting at Pier 2/63 offers excellent acoustics, as ell as concert-quality sound and ghting, for audiences of up to 4,000. No better setting to experience usic," is the verdict from *Rolling tone*. The 1999 lineup of performs included such luminaries as Chris aak, the Neville Brothers, and the ndigo Girls.

The company sponsors another local summer event—the AT&T Family Fourth at Lake Union—a unique blend of Asian and European fireworks set against the natural amphitheater surrounding Lake Union. Hundreds of thousands of people watch the annual display from the hills that circle the lake, and as many as 60,000 converge at Gas Works Park to take part in a free, daylong celebration of kids' activities, food, sports, and street performers. After the display is over, AT&T employees board kayaks and canoes and paddle through the lake, collecting debris.

Fireworks appear again at the end of each year with the AT&T New Year's at the Needle. The midnight display typically draws crowds in the tens of thousands.

In partnership with the Seattle Mariners, the company sponsors the annual Home Runs That Help program, which has raised $149,400 for Northwest charities since 1993. In 1999, the company donated $100 for every Mariner home run to Big Brothers and Big Sisters of King County, for a total of $24,400.

Demonstrating service in the interest of good corporate citizenship, AT&T Wireless Services remains firmly committed to the Seattle community. Through a civic-minded approach to doing business, the AT&T relationship with residents of the Pacific Northwest is a classic example of the perfect fit.

AT&T focuses on empowering communities by giving them the resources they need to improve health and human services, promote diversity, protect the environment, and stimulate volunteerism.

Boullioun Aviation Services, Inc.

In little more than a decade, Boulliou Aviation Services, Inc. has become one of the world's top three companies i the field of leasing commercial aircraft. With an aircraft portfolio wort approximately $2.4 billion, the company is headquartered in Bellevue, Washingto and has additional offices in Singapore and London. ● The compa atively new arena posed many initial challenges, but Boullioun positione itself to set the industry pace. President and CEO Robert Genise says, "We really have continued to build the business substantially." While leased aircraft currently represent about 20 percent of the aviation industry's global fleet, analysts expect that number to climb between 25 and 30 percent in a few years.

Boullioun's portion of that expanding market includes more than 200 aircraft owned, ordered, or optioned by the company and its affiliate in Singapore. Since 1995, Boullioun has placed 87 aircraft on lease with 40 airlines; concluded sale and leaseback contracts, and other back-to-back transactions, involving 29 aircraft; and sold 42 aircraft to airlines and investors. Transactions have been closed with a number of major airlines, including British Airways, America West, Alitalia, Air New Zealand, Emirates, Iberia, Korean Air, Malaysia Airlines, and Varig.

In little more than a decade, Boullioun Aviation Services, Inc. has become one of the world's top three companies in the field of leasing commercial aircraft.

Acquisition and Growth

In 1993, Boullioun cofounded Singapore Aircraft Leasing Enterprise Pte. Ltd. (SALE) with Singapore Airlines. Today, Singapore's major investment companies, Temasek Holdings and the Government of Singapore Investment Corporation, are also shareholders, each with a 14.5 percent holding. Boullioun acts as SALE's marketing representative worldwide.

Boullioun's Senior Management Team is (standing from left) Brad Johnson, Paul Dwyer, Chris Richards, Owen Roberts, John Willingham, Karla Showalter, (seated from left) Joel Hussey, Robert Genise, Tom Kaluza, Art Schmidt. Not pictured: Dave Walton, Kelly Grace

◄ Brant Photographers

In July 1998, Boullioun entered into an agreement to purchase up to 60 Boeing 737-700 aircraft to b delivered between 2001 and 2006. Of the total, half are firm orders an the rest are options, permitting th flexibility to switch to other mode

Boullioun was acquired in late 19 by the world's largest bank, Deutsc Bank AG, a global entity providin a broad range of banking, investme banking, and financial services throug out the world. Boullioun continue to function as an autonomous uni but the backing of Deutsche Bank provides it with tremendous financ firepower, a bonus for customers.

The co[illegible] announced its fi Airbus order in January 1999, agre ing to purchase 30 new A320 fami jetliners plus options. Deliveries beg in 2002 and will continue through 2006; the ultimate goal is a fleet o 250 aircraft in the portfolio. "With our current rate of growth, I think we can meet that goal in seven or eight years," says Genise.

Robert Genise, president and CEO of Boullioun, has more than 20 years of experience in the commercial aircraft leasing world.

namic Leadership

oullioun was founded in 1986 by E.H. "Tex" Boullioun, the ternationally renowned former esident of Boeing's Commercial irplane Group. Genise, who par- ered with Tex Boullioun in 1988, s 20 years of experience in the mmercial aircraft leasing world. ior to joining the company, he ent 11 years with Chemical Bank, here he ran a London-based special nance group focused exclusively international aircraft finance.

Genise's multiple degrees—a aster's degree in business from the niversity of Connecticut, a law gree from Pace University, and bachelor's degree in physics from ew York University (NYU)—re- ct a wide range of knowledge, but s heart is in the air. At NYU, he iginally intended to study aero- utics. "There's something about iation that fires the imagination," enise says.

xible Leasing

irline leasing requirements differ widely, based on criteria such as e destinations and routes an air- e flies, the makeu s existing ets, the strength of its financial sources, and the tax and account- g rules under which it operates. ullioun specializes in operating ses, which typically run from one ar to a decade. In an operating se, the lessee pays to use the air- aft during the lease term, but does t fully repay the lessor's investment and does not own the aircraft when the lease ends.

The attraction for airlines is plain—all the advantages of ownership with far fewer headaches. Leasing jetliners allows airlines to conserve valuable capital resources while reducing financial risk. It also provides carriers with the flexibility to fly a variety of aircraft that best meet changing operational and passenger needs.

With a global network of more than 50 employees who maintain constant contact with airlines, aircraft owners, and suppliers all over the world, Boullioun is well positioned to closely track today's fast-changing industry dynamics. Boullioun matches aircraft to customer needs, either from its own order book or from other sources, and then designs and executes flexible, creative lease deals that enable airlines to compete more effectively in their chosen markets.

Boullioun prides itself on personalized service and flexibility. Those qualities took center stage when a longtime customer, Virgin Express, sought to replace a Boullioun 737-300 with a 737-400 then available for lease. Such swaps are uncommon in the industry, but Boullioun was able to match the request with another customer, TAROM of Romania, which wished to add an additional 737-300. This level of commitment to its customers will ensure that the initial success of Boullioun Aviation Services, Inc. will continue to grow for decades to come.

▸ Watanabe Photography

With a global network of more than 50 employees who maintain constant contact with airlines, aircraft owners, and suppliers all over the world, Boullioun is well positioned to closely track today's fast-changing industry dynamics.

IT MAY NOT SOUND LIKE IT, BUT PLAYIN GAMES IS FAR FROM CHILD'S PLAY. THE NEW PARADIGM OF GAMING ENTERTAINMENT ATTRAC ADULTS AS WELL AS CHILDREN, AND CALLS FOR EVER MORE SOPHISTICATED BRANDS C IMMERSION. FROM POKÉMON TO MAGIC: THE GATHERING, WIZARDS OF THE COAST DETERMINED TO CAST A SPELL ON ADVENTURE SEEKERS OF ALL AGES. ● THE RENTON-BASE COMPANY, A SUBSIDIARY OF HASBRO, INC., IS THE WORLD'S LARGEST PUBLISHER C hobby games, a leading publisher of fantasy literature, and the owner of one of the nation's largest specialty game retail store chains. The firm employs approximately 2,000 people, with international offices in Antwerp, London, Paris, Beijing, and Milan.

The corporate environment of Wizards of the Coast is decidedly laid-back. Posters and action figures are everywhere, and the atmosphere crackles with the liveliness of youth. Many employees are gamers themselves, usually casually dressed and firing ideas between cubicles. It's not uncommon to see game designe Richard Garfield trading banter with researchers, or CEO Peter Adkison testing a game with other employees

Adkison received his degree in computer science from Walla Wall College in 1985. While still an employee of the Boeing Company, he founded Wizards of the Coast in 1990 with six other young professionals who had been creating and developing role-playing games in their spare time.

CRAIG CUDNOHUFSKY

CRAIG CUDNOHUFSKY

WIZARDS OF THE COAST'S RETAIL STORES ARE LOCATED ACROSS THE COUNTRY AND FEATURE UNIQUE GAME-PLAY SPACES (TOP).

IN 1999, THE POKÉMON TRADING CARD GAME MADE ITS AMERICAN DEBUT AND QUICKLY BECAME THE WORLD'S BEST-SELLING TRADING CARD GAME (BOTTOM).

Magic: The Gathering

Magic: The Gathering, a fantasy based trading card game intro duced in 1993, was the spark that brought the company internationa notoriety. In this intense game of strategy, players battle to reduce eac other's score from 20 to zero throug a series of attack and defense move wielding illustrated cards depicting fantastic monsters and imaginative worlds.

Devised by Garfield, the game initially sold 10 million cards in six weeks. It is now available in nine languages, sold in 52 countries, and played by more than 6 million peopl worldwide. Expansion packs with additional characters and plots are issued periodically and devoured b fans with all the fanfare of a major film release. The game has been extended to the PC, and has inspired a series of fantasy novels.

Continuing support for customers is a key aspect of the Wizards of th Coast philosophy. In addition to manufacturing games, the compan sponsors tournaments, contests, and other activities for gaming enthusiast Around the world, there are 1,600 Magic tournaments running each week, sanctioned by the company and, in some cases, backed by substantial prize money. Top players can receive as much as $25,000 for their skills.

CRAIG CUDNOHUFSKY

CRAIG CUDNOHUFSKY

Clockwise from top left: The Wizards of the Coast Game Center in the University District is one of the world's largest social, electronic, and computer game facilities in the world.

Thousands of kids show up in malls around the United States to learn to play the Pokémon trading card game.

Wizards of the Coast sponsors professional tournaments in locations around the world for its original trading card game, Magic: The Gathering.

"These organized play activities re a key component to our business," ays Carol Rogalski, director of orporate communications. "They epresent a fun and exciting social ctivity and provide people with ngoing opportunities to play ames with other game fans. We vant games to be a top-of-mind ntertainment choice for people."

laces to Play

Themes of social interaction extend to the company's retail game tores, a development dating to 1998. esides purchasing the latest releases rom game manufacturers, customrs can participate in competitive vents on-site, including multiplayer etwork matches for computer amers. The atmosphere of the tores evokes a vaguely medieval uality, with accents of mortar and nystery. "We don't just manufacure games," Rogalski says. "We reate places for people to play."

In 1997, the company opened the Vizards of the Coast Game Center, gaming entertainment center for ame enthusiasts, in Seattle's university istrict. The facility offers more than 50 games, a 3,800-square-foot video ame and pinball arcade, an 1,800-quare-foot retail store, a selection f networked computer games, a ,000-square-foot tournament cener for organized game play, and nultiple players' lounges.

ew Adventures

Dungeons and Dragons (D&D), the adventure game first made opular in the 1970s, also falls under he Wizards of the Coast library of games. The company acquired TSR, Inc., creators of D&D, in 1997. A reissue and boxed set of the game sold out within two months of its release. The company plans to release a new game revision—the first in 10 years—in the summer of 2000.

Another recent acquisition is The Game Keeper Inc., operator of 53 permanent retail stores and approximately 100 seasonal stores. Wizards of the Coast plans to bring social and competitive events to these sites in the near future.

On the publishing side, Wizards supports its products with several company-published magazines, including *TopDeck,* which began publishing in November 1999. The publication promises to be "an event in the gamer's mailbox each and every month," according to Johnny Wilson, group publisher of periodicals.

The company's latest adventures in gaming include the Pokémon trading card game, based on the popular series of video games by Nintendo and the animated television series. The game has already spawned trading card game leagues. Wizards of the Coast has broadened the trading card game genre to include other motifs, such as sports, comic-book superheroes, and World Championship Wrestling, and will soon include Harry Potter.

The end of 1999 saw another merchandising coup for the company—exclusive rights to publish role-playing games, tabletop games, and accessories based on the blockbuster *Star Wars* franchise. The first release of a *Star Wars*-based game product is scheduled for fall 2000.

According to Adkison, the Wizards of the Coast vision is to establish games as an intellectual, fun entertainment choice for people of all ages. It is achieving that goal by providing compelling adventures that challenge as well as entertain.

"Down through the ages it has come man's most divine heritage, the spirit of artistry," reads the flowery prose of the 1928 grand opening program of the Seattle Theatre, now known as The Paramount and one of Seattle's last remaining historic theaters. The program continues: "Ever inspiring, breaking the ties that bind, it has plotted the course of the centuries, marking the years with monuments of faith and beauty. Born in the heart of the earth, tempered by the travail of time out from the clay, the beginning, it bursts forth today in splendor and grandeur—a symbol of the world's newest art—the Seattle Theatre."

Built as a motion picture palace and vaudeville playhouse, the 3,000-seat theater, designed by legendary architect Marcus Priteca, was billed as the "largest and most beautiful theatre west of Chicago." The original program teased readers with high-powered coming attractions, including films starring Lon Chaney, Joan Crawford, and Clara Bow. The theater's opulence indicated the faith the so-called "mighty of the motion picture industry have in the future of Seattle."

Conceived and led by benefactress Ida Cole, the nonprofit Seattle Theatre Group was originally formed in 1992 as the Seattle Landmark Association. The group's leaders dedicated themselves to preserving the theater when its destruction appeared imminent. Since its $37 million renovation was completed, The Paramount has established itself as Seattle's premier performing arts entertainment venue, hosting a wide variety of arts programs, from touring Broadway musicals such as *Miss Saigon* to the theatrically driven rock of David Bowie.

"It's a passion that we have," says Patrick Harrison, director of marketing and communications for the Seattle Theatre Group. "Everyone here has a passion. We love the entertainment industry. Kafka said art and entertainment are the ax that breaks the cold heart."

The Seattle Theatre Group also handles booking and marketing for the Moore Theatre, the oldest remaining theater in Seattle. It was built in 1907 by James A. Moore, a flamboyant developer responsible for many of the early homes and structures in downtown Seattle and Capitol Hill. Renovated numerous times throughout the 20th century, the theater established Second Avenue as the city's film and theater district, and was the home to the first Seattle International Film Festival—now the nation's largest.

CLOCKWISE FROM TOP:
At the time of its construction, The Paramount was among the largest theaters of its type, built to accommodate stage acts, silent films, and organ and orchestral music.

Since its $37 million renovation was completed, The Paramount has established itself as Seattle's premier performing arts entertainment venue, hosting a wide variety of acts, from touring Broadway musicals such as *Miss Saigon* to the theatrically driven rock of David Bowie.

The Seattle Theatre Group also handles booking and marketing for the Moore Theatre, the oldest remaining theater in Seattle.

A Rich History Made Richer

At the time of its construction, The Paramount was among the largest theaters of its type, built to accommodate stage acts, silent films, and organ and orchestral music. Typical performance bills included live vaudeville entertainment, followed by a silent film with a mighty Wurlitzer organ accompaniment—an event that still takes place today

▶ PHIL BANKO

on Monday nights every summer. In The Paramount's early years, men and women of all ages and social backgrounds came to the theater day and night to revel in the glitter of Hollywood, watch Russian acrobats build human pyramids on stage, and hear the orchestra swing.

The theater's Wurlitzer organ, installed at an original cost of $100,000 (more than $1 million if done today), is a massive network of pipes, chimes, bells, whistles, and horns, with a built-in grand piano and drum set. Maintained by the Puget Sound Theatre Organ Society, it is one of only three such organs in the entire country that remain in their original theatrical home.

Decorative touches throughout the theater building bear the marks of craftsmanship and attention rarely seen today. Delicate ironwork curls into mermaids, and 218 chandeliers made of millions of individual glass beads glitter with light. To preserve this unique decor, seven decorative painters and plasterers worked for three months to restore the walls and ceilings. They restored 16 colors of paint and six decorative treatments in the grand lobby, using five glaze colors, six sponge treatments, six re-created plaster moldings, and 1,500 linear feet of foil.

The remodeling of the theater was closely monitored to match exact original specifications as much as possible. Colors and gold leaf designs were crafted to look as they did when the theater was constructed. At the same time, new air-conditioning systems were installed, electrical capacity was tripled, and acoustics were improved with modern retrofits.

Accommodating Performance

The original design of the theater, though well appointed, was not equipped to handle the elaborate mechanics and intricate technical demands of today's touring productions. The early vaudeville shows traveled light; all that was needed were a few props and the orchestra's instruments, which could be carried in through the stage door.

The Paramount features a high-tech structure that allows the theater to adjust to multiple types of performance in ways the original designers never imagined. A $5 million, convertible seating system and adjustable floor make it possible to transform the facility from a classical proscenium theater with 2,946 seats in a sloping house to a flat floor suitable for dinner, dancing, or private corporate events.

▶ PHIL BANKO

The remodeling of the theater was closely monitored to match exact original specifications as much as possible. Colors and gold leaf designs were crafted to look as they did when the theater was constructed.

Modern musicals, however, travel in multiple trailer trucks, which carry the sets and components that create onstage special effects. Prior to its renovation, The Paramount had a reputation for being one of the most inconvenient venues on the West Coast, because loading and unloading were so difficult.

Today, The Paramount features a new, high-tech structure that allows the theater to adjust to multiple types of performance in ways the original designers never imagined. A $5 million, convertible seating system and adjustable floor make it possible to transform the facility from a classical proscenium theater with 2,946 seats in a sloping house to a flat floor suitable for dinner, dancing, or private corporate events. The conversion process takes approximately three hours.

In addition, the entire back wall of the theater was removed during the recent renovation, and a new addition was constructed. The results were greater depth and wing space, making the theater large enough to accommodate modern stage productions. Dressing and costume rooms have been added, including a star dressing room, complete with a fireplace and Jacuzzi.

The theater also added a covered loading dock, solving the problem of trucks having to block the street during the loading and unloading processes. A new, larger box office was constructed, and 59 new bathroom stalls were added, as well as rest rooms accessible to the disabled on the first floor.

Tradition with Technology

Preserving tradition with an assist from today's technology, The Paramount broadcast the world's first Internet symphonic event, Cyberian Rhapsody, in 1995, as a benefit for United Way of King County. The Seattle Symphony, under the direction of conductor Gerard Schwarz, joined forces with several Seattle grunge bands in a world premiere of new music.

The Seattle Theatre Group uses its Web site, www.theparamount.com, as a forum to advertise upcoming events, promote subscriptions to any of its six seasons of entertainment, sell tickets, and market the theater as a site for private events and corporate gatherings. The site includes a virtual tour of the theater, complete with a wealth of details with regard to the renovation process.

Education

Essential to the Seattle Theatre Group is the provision of year-round educational opportunities that promote creative experiences and partnerships within the community, as well as provide training for young artists in dance, music, and theater. Started in 1999, Dance This features traditional and contemporary youth dance groups at the Moore Theatre. Diverse dance companies participate in weeklong cross-cultural workshops held each summer, as well as performing for youth and family audiences.

Dance With Us offers master classes, lectures, demonstrations, and performances with national and international touring companies featured in the theater's dance season. The Art of Musicals series targets high school drama classes, and includes performances, workshops, meet-the-artist programs, and backstage tours.

Music Sound Checks invites young musicians to sound checks and question-and-answer sessions with touring groups in association with the National Academy of Recording Arts and Sciences. The theater also offers pre-film lectures prior to Silent Movie Mondays, as well as More Music @ The Moore, targeting young musicians in a range of styles through workshops and a performance series.

Since 1992, the Seattle Theatre Group has been at the forefront of providing an outstanding mix of events and performances for the Seattle area. As it has in the past, the theater will continue to enrich and educate the members of the community it serves, both young and old.

Decorative touches throughout the theater building bear the marks of craftsmanship and attention rarely seen today.

COVERING THE COMPANIES, PERSONALITIES, RENDS, AND ISSUES THAT ARE SHAPING THE CHARACTER AND FUTURE OF THE STATE'S CONOMY, *Washington CEO Magazine* IS FULFILLING ITS EDITORIAL MISSION TO BE HE BUSINESS MAGAZINE OF WASHINGTON STATE. AFTER A DECADE OF PUBLISHING, THE OUR-COLOR MONTHLY HAS ESTABLISHED ITSELF AS THE AREA'S LEADING FORUM FOR THE XCHANGE OF BUSINESS AND ECONOMIC IDEAS. ● THE MAGAZINE IS THE FLAGSHIP OF ublisher Scott Fivash. His commitment to a high-quality editorial roduct is reflected in a staff of writers nd editors with years of experience the competitive arena of Puget ound journalism.

Serving an audience of about ○,000 chief executive officers, comany presidents, business owners, and ntrepreneurs, *Washington CEO* is tuned to the pulse of the region's ommerce. The magazine's readers re powerful, influential, educated, nd established members of the busiess community. As *Washington EO* has evolved, the magazine has ecome both a resource for learning bout regional business trends and way to gain insight into the personities shaping the region's economy.

Washington CEO's readers appreate the magazine's insightful writing, lid reporting, and knack for knowg what's around the corner. In each sue, the editors of *Washington CEO* ffer stories on prominent business aders, maverick approaches to probm solving, overviews of important statewide industries, and successful turnarounds.

A Signature of Quality

One of the company's signature features throughout the past decade is the annual Best Companies to Work For in Washington state issue. The list has included such local luminaries as AT&T Wireless, Attachmate, and the Frank Russell Co. As Fivash notes, the idea of recognizing employee-friendly companies has taken hold in national publications such as *Fortune* and *Inc.*, which now publish annual lists of their own.

"We hope that these ideas rub off on a few others, contributing in our effort to make Washington state one of the best places to work," Fivash writes. "We are also encouraged that some of this 'best companies to work for' thinking is rubbing off on our own company, as we at *Washington CEO* continually seek to readjust and improve the way we do business."

Washington CEO was named a Gold Award Winner for Best Regional Business Magazine in the Nation by *Folio:* in its 1998 Editorial Excellence Awards. "Packed with information, *Washington CEO* should be on the 'must-read' list for every member of the state's business economy," the judges wrote. The magazine was also the 1995 winner of the Western Publications Association Maggie Award for best business magazine. *Washington CEO*'s editor, Peter Santucci, recently received the silver award for editorial excellence for his *Inklings* column from the American Society of Business Press Editors.

In addition, *Washington CEO* hosts roughly six events each year such as the Economic Forecast Breakfast and the E-commerce Summit, which collectively draw about 2,000 top Washington state executives.

With a focus on a quality editorial product and a readership comprised of the state's best and brightest, *Washington CEO* will continue its contribution to business in the Pacific Northwest for years to come.

INSIGHTFUL AND IN-DEPTH IN ITS REPORTING, *WASHINGTON CEO MAGAZINE*'S AWARD-WINNING COVERAGE EXTENDS FROM BILL GATES TO ITS ANNUAL BEST COMPANIES TO WORK FOR, MAKING IT REQUIRED READING FOR BUSINESS SUCCESS IN WASHINGTON STATE.

THE SIMPLICITY OF THE CITY CHURCH' NAME IS OFFSET BY THE COMPLEXITY OF ITS QUEST—A COMMITMENT TO CHRISTIANITY FUTURE AS WELL AS ITS PAST. "I THINK WE WOULD CONSIDER OURSELVES 21ST-CENTURY CHURCH," SAYS PASTOR WENDELL SMITH, FOUNDER OF KIRKLAND-BASE CITY CHURCH. "OUR APPROACHES ARE FRESH AND, PERHAPS TO SOME PEOPLE, NOVE AT THE SAME TIME, THEY ARE BUILT ON A FOUNDATION OF WHAT WE SEE I first-generation Christianity." Those approaches include programs designed to appeal to contemporary Christians—youth church, drama, banquets, conferences, classes, City Kids, and guest speakers contribute to a modern church community.

The church underscores its commitment to diversity within its stated mission "to build a New Testament local church and proclaim the good news about Jesus Christ to young and old, rich and poor, red and yellow, black and white, and extend the kingdom of God by building people, families, and leaders—first in our city, and then in the ends of the earth."

A Church for Everyone

An emphasis on diversity and youth is central to the church's efforts. Smith describes the church as multidenominational, drawing inspiration from the evangelical charismatic tradition. Approximately 700 young people—ranging from junior high to college age—gather together each week in a dynamic ministry called Generation Church. A separate ministry aimed at children is called City Kids, and has a membe ship of about 350.

"The church has become an expression of more than 50 different nations and nationalities," says Smith. "There is quite a racial diversity."

SINCE ITS FOUNDING IN 1992, THE CITY CHURCH HAS GROWN TO BECOME THE SPIRITUAL HOME OF MORE THAN 3,000 PEOPLE.

FOUNDED BY WENDELL AND GINI SMITH, CITY CHURCH EMPHASIZES BOTH YOUTH AND DIVERSITY, UTILIZING PROGRAMS SUCH AS GENERATION CHURCH AND CITY KIDS—DESIGNED TO APPEAL TO CONTEMPORARY CHRISTIANS.

'he church places high priority on ɔcial service and assistance to those ı need. Through a program called ıe City Ministries, the church feeds ıore than 15,000 people a week with food distribution network targeting ɔartment complexes in the commu- ity. Social service efforts are operated ɔoperatively, in collaboration with ɔ different churches throughout ıe Seattle area.

"We have clothing distribution," ıys Smith. "We own a large ware- ouse where we receive food and lothing from a variety of vendors nd companies, and we pass that long to people in need. That has een a tremendous blessing, not nly to the people who are receiving , but also to the people who have een involved in the distribution rocess. It's a wonderful thrill."

The City Church has all of the allmarks of a thoroughly modern ıinistry, but at the same time, the hurch incorporates many time- onored traditions into its services. ⁄lusic and singing are integral to ⁄orship services, as is anointed reaching.

hree Decades of Ministry

Wendell Smith and his wife, Gini, also a pastor, were mar- ied in 1972. Wendell's roots in the rea stretch to Tacoma, where he ⁄as born in 1950. Both of his parents ⁄ere pastors, and he inherited their ift, beginning preaching at age 16.

For 20 years, Wendell and Gini mith were members of City Bible Church in Portland, Oregon, for- ıerly known as Bible Temple. In ɔ92, the Smiths decided to launch a new church in the Northwest.

The effort began during the spring and summer of that year. The first interest meeting for the church was held in May at Camp Sambica at Lake Sammamish, in Washington State, with 40 people in attendance. By August, official Sunday services were under way in a pair of conference rooms at the Bellevue Courtyard Marriott Hotel.

Subsequently, the church moved into its first true home, at Bellevue's Kelsey Creek Center, signing a five-year lease. By 1996, attendance was averaging 1,000 per month at week-end services, and the Kelsey Creek Center location was beginning to get cramped.

The City Church continued to grow, and in late 1997, the church found a home in a facility purchased from the neighboring Overlake Christian Church. The spacious complex on Rose Hill—along the boundaries of Kirkland and Redmond—is bordered by a stand of the Puget Sound region's ubiquitous Douglas firs. The first services at the new location generated attendance of more than 1,400. Now, more than 3,000 call The City Church home.

The church's name is borrowed in part from the Book of Isaiah, which speaks of "the city of righteousness, the faithful city." But Smith looks to another passage for inspiration.

"The biblical phrase 'Cast your net on the other side' has been kind of a hallmark that has led our church," Smith says. "Our focus as a church has been to minister not only to people's spiritual needs, but also to physical needs as part of the commission of Christ to our world."

Covenant Celebration Church

For senior pastors Kevin and Sheil Gerald and the 5,000-plus members of Covenant Celebration Church, succes begins on Sunday. "People who go to work Monday through Friday believ success starts with the workweek," explains Kevin Gerald, who helped foun Covenant Celebration Church in 1993. "We believe God comes first and tha success in life really begins on Sunday. That's why we've made it our motto.

For senior pastors Kevin and Sheila Gerald and the 5,000-plus members of Covenant Celebration Church, success begins on Sunday.

Covenant Celebration was born out of a marriage between People's Church, a 1,200-member church in Tacoma, and Meridian Christian Ministries in Puyallup. Located on a 21-acre campus in South Tacoma, Covenant Celebration Church is one of the largest churches in the Northwest, and offers attendees everything from one-on-one training and small group experiences to large venue worship activities and performances.

Something for Everyone

Covenant Celebration's burgundy-and-cream-colored sanctuary feels cozy even though it seats close to 3,000 worshipers. It features four big-screen televisions and two giant screens, a stage, and a generous choir loft for the admired and talented Celebration Choir and Praise Team. With two services on Sunday, one service on Wednesday night, and Kevin Gerald's television program, *Wisdom for Life,* airing on Seattle's KONG-TV and the Sky Angel Network, Covenant Celebration has something for everyone.

Also on tap are a variety of small group studies for people—whether they are new believers, seasoned Christians, or somewhere in between. Covenant Celebration has a full-service Christian bookstore on the premises, and there are also men's and women's groups, as well as children's and youth activities.

Children and youth are, in fact, a celebrated part of Covenant Celebration. The church is in the process of building a 40,000-square-foot building, Champions Centre, just for them. The building will offer an 800-seat auditorium, as well as numerous rooms serving as both classroom and meeting space. A youth café and bookstore will also be provided, along with donated equipment from a nearby Discovery Zone that recently closed.

For those who would like to get a little deeper into the faith, Kevin Gerald Communications, a series of books and audiotapes, speaks to a wide range of interests. Gerald's most well known book is *The Proving Ground,* a 107-page volume that provides nine tests to prove personal potential. Gerald has also authored *Pardon Me, I'm Prospering*; *Developing Confidence*; *Characteristics of a Winner*; *Raising Champion Children*; and other volumes.

Covenant Celebration's umbrell outreach organization, Impact, supports a series of programs that serve the community, such as the Tacom Rescue Mission, Operation Hope, Family Renewal Shelter, and Wings Life Skills Training—a 40-hour class that teaches those at the bottom of the economic ladder how to develop

Covenant Celebration's sanctuary seats close to 3,000 worshipers, and includes a loft for the Celebration Choir and Praise Team.

Covenant Celebration has resurrected the time-honored practice of ministry through drama.

ɔnfidence, adopt a positive attitude overcome their adversities, and cus on a better life.

ıurch Leadership Training

or those pursuing the ministry as a full-time profession, Covenant elebration's Wisdom for Life School Ministries (not to be confused with e church's television show of the me name) provides a supplement seminary training. While seminaries ɔcus on the theological and theo- tical underpinnings of the ministry, Visdom for Life focuses on the practi- ıl, everyday aspects of the ministry, such as counseling people in economic and spiritual crises.

The two-year Wisdom for Life course offers an integrated program of biblical studies, theology, church leadership, and ministry training, with an emphasis on leadership and training. Wisdom for Life trains leaders to be culturally relevant while remaining anchored to the timeless truth of the Bible.

Ministry through Drama

The tradition of ministry through drama is a time-honored practice that reaches back to the Middle Ages, when churches presented so-called mystery plays based on the Gospels. Covenant Celebration has resurrected this method and given it new life. The church's two major drama productions are famous in the Pacific Northwest.

One of Covenant Celebration's annual productions is *Jesus of Nazareth*, a scripture-based production of the life of Jesus performed with the help of a cast and crew of more than 1,000 people from 25 different churches, plus live animals including camels, sheep, and horses. For more than 20 years, *Jesus of Nazareth* has been staged at the amphitheatre in Puyallup. More than 35,000 people attend the production, which runs from July to August.

Scrooge the Musical is Covenant Celebration's other signature event. More than 20,000 people attend this unique look at *A Christmas Carol*, the classic Charles Dickens tale, held every December in the church's sanctuary.

Today, through Gerald's leadership, Covenant Celebration is going strong. The decision to unite two churches in the name of putting God first was clearly the right one. According to Marketing Director Tinia Nelson, "We're one big happy family. This is a great place to be."

For more than 20 years, *Jesus of Nazareth* has been staged at the amphitheatre in Puyallup. More than 35,000 people attend the production, which runs from July to August.

IN THE EARLY YEARS OF THE INTERNET BOO AUDIO AND VIDEO FILES, OFTEN HEAVY WITH GRAPHIC DATA, WERE DIFFICULT TO LOAD. IN SENSE, THE INTERNET WAS MUTE. AUDIO FILES HAD TO BE COMPLETELY DOWNLOADED BEFO THEY COULD BE HEARD, AND THE AMOUNT OF TIME IT TOOK TO RECEIVE A FILE EXCEEDED T AMOUNT OF TIME IT TOOK TO LISTEN TO IT BY A RATIO OF 5-TO-1 OR HIGHER. ● BORN 1994 AS THE PIONEER IN MEDIA DELIVERY ON THE INTERNET, REALNETWORKS®, IN develops and markets software products and services designed to enable users of personal computers and other consumer electronic devices to send and receive audio, video, and other multimedia services using the Web. Today, consumers can easily access and experience audio/video programming and download RealNetworks' consumer software on the Internet at www.real.com.

RealNetworks, Inc., founded by CEO Rob Glaser (right), is the leading developer and distributor of audio and video media delivery systems for the Internet.

RealNetworks, the trailblazer of audio compression, broke the Internet "sound barrier" in 1995 with the introduction of RealAudio®. This changed the landscape of the Internet, establishing a new paradigm of quality and positioning the company as a financial force to be reckoned with. In 1997, RealNetworks further propelled the Internet media revolution with the introduction of RealVideo®. RealNetworks continually refines and improves its audio and video products to drive the evolution of the digital media industry.

As of 1999, RealNetworks had nearly 800 employees. Robust revenue growth has made the company a favorite among market watchers; the company's revenues for the first quarter of 2000 rose to $53.5 million—an increase of 120 percent from the previous year.

Innovative Leadership

The heart and soul of RealNetworks is its founder and CEO, Rob Glaser. Armed with bachelor's and master's degrees in economics, a bachelor's degree in computer science from Yale University, and 10 years of experience at Microsoft, Glaser has long been intrigued by the nexu of media, computing, and communication. As television and radio shi from a broadcast to an on-line medium, Glaser envisions turning the Internet into the next mass medium

Glaser is committed to community support as well as the progress c his company. He serves on several nonprofit boards and committees, including the Advisory Committee on Public Interest Obligations of Digital Television Broadcasters, an appointment he received from President Bill Clinton.

Accelerated Adoption of Consumer Products

RealNetworks, has in only a few short years, cultivated incredible momentum on many fronts. It signature product, RealPlayer®, is the world's most popular Internet audio and video player, with more than 140 million unique registered users as of August 2000. Recognizing the varied needs of its consumers, RealNetworks has developed rsions of RealPlayer that have been apted to Unix, Macintosh, and indows users.

The commitment to versatility s paid off. According to Nielsen// etRatings, there are currently more S. home users of RealPlayer than the two largest competing media ayers combined. RealJukebox™, troduced in May 1999, is the most pular music jukebox software in the untry, with more than 40 million ique registered users as of August oo. Consumers have already used alJukebox to play or record more an 1 billion songs.

Leading the digital distribution arket, RealNetworks has developed alJukebox as the first universal digital usic system. RealNetworks provides pport for all leading music formats for ayback in RealJukebox—including P3, RealAudio, AT&T's a2b, IBM's MMS, Liquid Audio, Mjuice, Sony usic's ATRAC3, and Universal usic Group/InterTrust—giving nsumers access to the broadest array music on the Web.

Agreements with AOL, Apple, atsushita (Panasonic), Nokia, Intel, ny Electronics, Universal Music roup, and others demonstrate the iquity of RealNetworks' Internet media delivery platform, and extend the availability of digital media to new mediums.

Leveraging Distribution

Demonstrating the distribution and promotional strength of RealNetworks' products and services, Real.com™ Network was launched to better connect consumers to content. Real.com Network's sites, which include Real.com Take5™, Real.com Guide, channels, live stations, Real.com Message Service, and other products and services, command impressive distribution. Traffic to Real.com Guide grew by more than 78 percent among home users in the first six months of 2000, according to Nielsen//NetRatings. Since the introduction of Real.com Guide in November 1999, RealNetworks has driven an estimated 430 million visits to media companies providing programming through Real.com Network.

Further demonstrating the reach of Real.com Network, RealNetworks downloaded more than 62 million unique software packages to consumers in the first quarter of 2000, an increase of 175 percent from a year earlier.

RealNetworks continues to stay abreast of new developments in the technology landscape. In early 2000, the company acquired privately held Netzip, Inc., a leading developer and provider of Internet download management and utility software. Another development has been the launch of Real.com Games, offering a new, online digital distribution model for high-quality downloadable and online PC games.

RealNetworks' recognized leadership in broadband Internet media delivery was further solidified with the adoption of broadband-ready RealSystem® G2 by Akamai, Cidera, iBeam, InterPacket, and PanAmSat, joining leading broadcast providers such as Digital Island, Enron Broadband Services, Globix, Intervu, and Madge.web to deliver the highest-quality broadband Internet media to mass audiences worldwide.

With so many competitors in such a cutting-edge industry, RealNetworks has proved itself an enduring leader through innovation and acumen. Through the vision of its leader and the desire to remain at the forefront of audio and video transmission, the company is poised for continued success in the decades to come.

As of 1999, RealNetworks had nearly 800 employees. Robust revenue growth has made the company a favorite among market watchers; the company's revenues for the first quarter of 2000 rose to $53.5 million—an increase of 120 percent from the previous year.

Western Wireless Corporation/VoiceStream Wireless Corporation

MORE THAN 100 MILLION AMERICANS CU RENTLY OWN WIRELESS PHONES, YET THE WIRELESS INDUSTRY IS FAR FROM REACHING ITS FU POTENTIAL. THE PERSONAL COMMUNICATIONS INDUSTRY ASSOCIATION PREDICTS THAT NE PERSONAL COMMUNICATIONS SERVICES WILL COMBINE WITH EXISTING WIRELESS SERVIC SUCH AS CELLULAR AND PAGING TO FUNDAMENTALLY CHANGE THE WAY AMERICANS COMMU NICATE. ● RECOGNIZING THE POTENTIAL OF MARKETS THAT HAVE BEEN HISTORICALL underserved, Western Wireless Corporation (Nasdaq:WWCA) is a leading provider of communications in rural America. Headquartered in Bellevue, Washington, Western Wireless owns and operates wireless cellular phone systems marketed under the Cellular One® brand name in 19 states west of the Mississippi River, covering about 25 percent of the land in the continental United States with a combined population of approximately 9 million people. Through the second quarter of 2000, Western Wireless/Cellular One provided service to more than 930,500 customers.

WITH THE RICH BLEND OF SERVICES IT OFFERS, WESTERN WIRELESS CORPORATION IS COMMITTED TO BECOMING THE NATION'S PREMIER RURAL COMMUNICATIONS PROVIDER. THE COMPANY'S MISSION IS FOCUSED ON THREE IDEALS: QUALITY, GROWTH, AND PROFITABILITY.

Western Wireless was formed in July 1994, through the merger of Pacific Northwest Cellular and General Cellular Corporation. Since then, the company has grown from approximately 320 employees to more than 2,000. In May 1996, the company completed an initial public offering of 12.65 million shares of common stock and a public bond offering.

The two offerings raised nearly $430 million in net proceeds to continue the development of the company's cellular and other communications businesses. In addition to the cellular business, Western Wireless also offers residential long-distance, wireless residential, paging, data, and competitive local exchange carrier (CLEC) services.

With the rich blend of services it offers, Western Wireless is committed to becoming the nation's premier rural communications provider. The company's mission is focused on three ideals: quality, growth, and profitability. Western Wireless is dedicated to expanding the firm's business through providing superior systems and service, earning customer loyalty, providing excellent customer care, and effecting prudent acquisitions. This goal helps the company deliver on its commitment to provide outstanding return on investment to shareholders. By continuing to concentrate on being nimble and entrepreneurial, Western Wireless is poised for future success in the competiti and dynamic communications industry.

Getting More from VoiceStream

Also headquartered in Bellevue, VoiceStream Wireless Corporatic (Nasdaq: VSTR) is a leading provid of digital wireless communications in the United States, utilizing the globa system for mobile communications (GSM) technology, the world's mo widely used digital standard. After th Federal Communications Commissio (FCC) auctions of broadband person communications system (PCS) licens in 1995, 1997, and 1999, Western Wireless acquired PCS licenses through its VoiceStream Wireless subsidiary.

Spun off from Western Wireless in 1999, VoiceStream continues to aggressively develop its network an presence in North America. Throug a series of successful mergers and acquisitions, VoiceStream has grow to become a major nationwide provider of wireless communications services and the largest GSM operato worldwide.

Since 1998, actress Jamie Lee Curti has been VoiceStream's spokesperson

SPUN OFF FROM WESTERN WIRELESS IN 1999, VOICESTREAM WIRELESS CORPORATION IS A LEADING PROVIDER OF DIGITAL WIRELESS COMMUNICATIONS IN THE UNITED STATES. JOHN W. STANTON IS CHAIRMAN AND CEO OF BOTH WESTERN WIRELESS AND VOICESTREAM.

troducing the company's popular Get More business philosophy nationwide. By offering customers more minutes, more features, and more service than any other wireless provider in the market, VoiceStream has become the fastest-growing wireless provider in the country.

Consistent with the company's Get More strategy, VoiceStream offers a variety of wireless services, freeing customers to get more from life with their personal time and the money they save. VoiceStream offers wireless Internet services through a personal portal called MyVoicestream.com, successfully integrating Internet functionality with wireless service in a manner that complements both technologies and provides a superior customer experience. Two-way e-mail lets customers send and receive e-mail using a wireless device—filtering, forwarding, and replying to a home or office e-mail address via their wireless phone.

Additionally, customers can receive stock prices, sports scores, daily horoscopes, weather updates, and other news services directly to their handsets. VoiceStream will continue to expand these services by adding e-commerce and high-speed Internet browsing using wireless access protocol (WAP) and hypertext markup language (HTML) enabled handsets.

VoiceStream has a significant presence throughout the state of Washington, both as a service provider and as a major employer. The company provides service to all cities along the I-5 corridor from the Canadian border to Cottage Grove, Oregon, as well as the Greater Spokane area through Sandpoint, Idaho. VoiceStream also operates a 51,000-square-foot customer care center in Bellingham, and employs some 1,200 employees throughout the state.

A proven leader in the field of digital wireless services, VoiceStream will continue to expand its services with a focus on delivering the best value in wireless communications across the state and across the country.

Leadership in Action

In a world of perpetual motion and change, one thing remains constant in both the Western Wireless and VoiceStream worlds. At the helm of both ships is John W. Stanton, chairman, director, and CEO of both companies. Stanton, also a cofounder of McCaw Cellular Communications, is regarded as both a leader and a visionary in the wireless industry. Stanton's astute deal making and steadfast delivery have earned him both the respect and the backing of major international players, and have placed his young companies on the national stage.

Named *Puget Sound Business Journal*'s 1999 Executive of the Year, Stanton continues to post some of the best numbers in the wireless industry for both companies. With a rich blend of rural and urban communication strategies, Stanton is poised to take Western Wireless and VoiceStream to the highest levels of success well into the next century.

By continuing to concentrate on being nimble and entrepreneurial, Western Wireless is poised for future success in the competitive and dynamic communications industry.

Since 1998, actress Jamie Lee Curtis has been VoiceStream's spokesperson, introducing the company's popular Get More business philosophy nationwide.

Wade Cook Financial Corporation

WADE COOK FINANCIAL CORPORATION, INC (WCFC), ONE OF THE NATION'S LEADERS IN FINANCIAL EDUCATION, OFFERS INDIVIDUA INVESTORS A WEALTH OF PRODUCTS AND SERVICES DESIGNED TO TEACH UNIQUE TRADIN STRATEGIES FOR GENERATING MONTHLY INCOME AND PROMOTING WEALTH ENHANCEMEN THE COMPANY CONDUCTS EDUCATIONAL SEMINARS, PRODUCES AND SELLS VIDEO- AND AUDIC TAPES, AND DISTRIBUTES BOOKS AND OTHER WRITTEN MATERIALS, ALL OF WHICH FOCUS O financial and personal wealth creation strategies.

In addition, WCFC operates several publishing subsidiaries that produce books, manuals, and other written materials relating to personal finance, inspirational themes, and other topics. The company also provides subscription-based Internet access and paging services, and maintains an information network on the Internet. Additional WCFC investments include ownership of minority interests in hotels, marketable securities, real estate, oil and gas, and other venture capital partnerships and private companies.

WCFC has a highly skilled team of more than 300 employees, including some 250 full-time and 65 part-time employees, as well as approximately 50 independent contractors providing professional speaking services. An extensive training program provides employees and speakers with special techniques to enhance the value of their services.

WADE COOK FINANCIAL CORPORATION PROVIDES A COMPLETE RANGE OF EDUCATIONAL PRODUCTS AND SERVICES DESIGNED TO TEACH STRATEGIES AND TECHNIQUES FOR GENERATING MONTHLY INCOME AND PROMOTING WEALTH ENHANCEMENT.

A Determined, Down-to-Earth Founder

Company founder Wade B. Cook was born in Tacoma to a working-class family. Always determined to blaze his own trail, Cook worked as a cabdriver and ran his own businesses. As he began to explore the world of investing, Cook soon learne how to make his money work for him instead of working for his money. Using his hard-won experience and knowledge, he wrote a series of finan cial best-sellers, including *Real Estat Money Machine* and *Wall Street Money Machine*, which propelled him into a new career in financial seminars.

A MOTIVATOR, AN EDUCATOR, A BUSINESS EXECUTIVE, AND A CHRISTIAN, WADE COOK USES HIS KNOWLEDGE AND INSIGHT TO TEACH HIS PUPILS HOW TO MAKE THEIR MONEY WORK FOR THEM, INSTEAD OF SIMPLY WORKING FOR THEIR MONEY.

An educator, business executive, stock market investor, and motivational speaker, Cook is also a down to-earth individual who doesn't minc telling people that he is a Christian. For example, one of his best-sellers, *Business Buy the Bible*, discusses financial principles in a faith-based context.

Cook is also a man who believes in heeding the wisdom of those wh have come before him. He is fond o motivational quotes, sprinkling then throughout his lectures and relying on them as an effective means of expressing fundamental principles. He has even compiled a collection o his favorite quotes, the best-selling *Wade Cook's Power Quotes.*

Cook recognizes the significance of the growing generation of stock market investors who are extremely active. According to the Federal Reserve Board, the value of household

WCFC understands that people want to increase their wealth by increasing their cash flow, minimizing state and federal taxes, protecting their assets, and retiring with sufficient income to maintain a comfortable standard of living.

›rporate equity holdings has in-:eased from $903 billion in 1980 to 4.78 trillion in 1996. Furthermore, 1999, the Federal Reserve estimated ıat 28 percent of household wealth ı the United States was in the form f stock investments, a figure up 12 ercent from 1990. WCFC believes ıis growth is due to population in-:eases within the United States, the ct that the baby boom generation is ıtering midlife, the prolonged growth f the U.S. economy during the 990s, and the recent growth in the ıarket value of corporate securities.

With this information in mind, 'CFC has based most of its pro-:ams, products, and services on the ıancial and trading strategies of its ›under. Cook believes that as part f this new generation of investors, eople want to learn to increase their ealth by increasing their cash flow, ıinimize their federal and state income taxes, protect their assets, retire with sufficient income to maintain a comfortable standard of living, and pass on their accumulated wealth to their loved ones.

WCFC's goal is to teach its students to accomplish these goals through clear, concise, and empowering education. The company's stated business plan is "to provide the best possible stock market and financial education available in America today and continue to grow and expand our core business of financial education by adjusting and adapting to the constant flux of the market and bringing our innovation to America."

SMILe

WCFC provides a wealth of services and products to customers through multiple divisions, and creates interest and demand for its programs, products, and services through a mix of radio and television advertising, direct mail, trade shows, Internet marketing, flyers, sports promotion, billboard advertising, and sponsorship of charitable organizations. A group of corporate components and programs—including the Stock Market Institute of Learning, Inc. (SMILe) and Semper Financial, Inc.—deliver the firm's products to individual customers.

SMILe represents a major segment of the company's educational effort. Providing comprehensive education on stock market trading strategies, the institute holds various seminars and clinics in the nation's most populous cities on topics relating to the stock market and wealth enhancement. SMILe also produces and sells home study courses that teach students specialized and innovative strategies to improve their trading skills.

In 1999 alone, WCFC held 2,700 SMILe seminars throughout the United States on topics aimed at generating perpetual monthly income and empowering Americans with important knowledge and the tools for achieving financial freedom.

THROUGH THE PROGRAMS OFFERED BY SMILE AND SEMPER FINANCIAL, WCFC DEVELOPS STRONG CUSTOMER RELATIONSHIPS THAT ARE UNIQUE IN THE SEMINAR INDUSTRY.

In 1999 alone, WCFC held 2,700 SMILe seminars throughout the United States on topics aimed at generating monthly income and empowering Americans with important knowledge and the tools for achieving financial freedom. All combined, more than 100,000 people attended these events. SMILe is currently developing a number of new and innovative seminars, which the institute believes will provide added financial stability in the future.

Individual SMILe seminar topics, which are usually developed by Cook himself, reflect a wide range of approaches to investing. They include the Financial Clinic™, the Wall Street Workshop™ (WSWS), and Youth Wall Street™, among others.

The Financial Clinic is a two-and-a-half-hour seminar that explains the financial education products and services offered by SMILe. The clinic provides an introduction to strategies for investing in the stock market, including rolling stock, covered calls, and options. WSWS is a two-day seminar that teaches students how to create income using specific stock market strategies. WSWS students are taught basic stock market termi nology and stock market strategies. The workshop features instruction strategy demonstrations, and exten sive practice through paper trades.

Youth Wall Street is a version o WSWS for teenagers. The seminar focuses on teaching youth how the financial markets work and how the can experience the market themselv by making trades on paper. WCFC often offers free admission to the Youth Wall Street workshop to hig school business clubs and similar groups as a community service. As part of its youth program, the com pany helps schools establish investment clubs and provides them wit the information needed to run the clubs effectively. WCFC also provid presentations and special seminars for the benefit of the clubs.

Semper Financial, Inc.

In January 1999, WCFC launche Semper Financial, Inc. to comple ment its services and to expand its market share in the seminar industr Semper Financial hosts a three-day convention where attendees are exposed to a number of strategies an concepts taught by 18 to 20 proficie speakers in their respective fields. Attendees who wish to learn more

bout the concepts are encouraged attend the SMILe seminars that re appropriate to their interests.

Semper Financial is proving to be n asset to WCFC. In its first year, emper Financial held 10 conventions various locations across the United tates, including Orlando, Las Vegas, nd Dallas, and built a customer base f more than 8,200 individuals. The onventions generally attracted large rowds, with some events seeing ttendance levels as high as 1,200 eople. In addition to generating evenues for the company, Semper inancial has aided in the development of brand awareness for VCFC's products and services.

Based on the success of the 1999 schedule, WCFC planned several additional Semper Financial seminars for 2000 and 2001. The company also plans to add a similar, one-day event called Prime Seminars, which will feature three to four speakers who are experts in their particular strategies.

Telling, Showing, Doing

Through the programs offered by SMILe and Semper Financial, WCFC develops strong customer relationships that it believes are unique in the seminar industry. Students benefit from a type of instruction that is not offered anywhere else; this type of financial education, which specializes in increasing cash flow, is unavailable through most financial institutions today. While some financial institutions offer clients limited education, they rarely inform their clients of the variety of trading choices available to them in the market.

WCFC students, however, are empowered with the tools necessary to trade successfully, as well as with the confidence and know-how to minimize their risks. Whether novices, intermediate learners, or advanced traders, students first contact WCFC through its enrollment directors, who help them navigate the many products and services, and try to find a fit for their educational needs. Next, students are initiated into the company's educational

WCFC MAINTAINS A HIGHLY ACTIVE PUBLISHING ARM THAT HAS PRODUCED SUCH BEST-SELLING TITLES AS *WALL STREET MONEY MACHINE*, *STOCK MARKET MIRACLES*, AND *BUSINESS BUY THE BIBLE*.

WCFC SPONSORS *EXPLANATIONS*, A NEWSLETTER THAT PROVIDES SUBSCRIBERS WITH CONTINUING EDUCATION ABOUT THE STOCK MARKET AND THE COMPANY'S TRADING STRATEGIES.

materials through a format that is both supportive and extremely accessible. Students then learn the appropriate vocabulary, study the fundamentals of various trading strategies, and receive demonstrations of ways to put their newly gained education into action.

One of WCFC's secrets to success in this field lies in the company's teaching methods, based on a unique blend of experiential and rote learning that makes its educational process truly one of a kind. Cook's signature strategy is the tell–show–do educational format. "First, we tell you the method for placing a trade using the vocabulary that brokers understand," Cook says. "Second, we show you how a trade is done by doing simulated live trades. Third and finally, we break and allow the students to do a trade for themselves, either real or on paper. It's that simple.

"As simple as it sounds, our method is unique in the financial education industry," says Cook. "We go into the detailed aspects of the trades to educate students about who plays a role with each step of their trades, who gets a share of the money they spent to get the trades done, and where along the path the trades are actually sent to the floor for execution."

After students are inducted into the learning process, the company's staff of highly trained enrollment representatives guides them through their continuing educational needs. WCFC does not see its role in the student's life as that of a casual retailer, but rather as a companion and resource to be called upon while the student is on the road to financial independence.

Publishing Best-Sellers

WCFC also maintains a highly active publishing arm, made u of four unique publishers and a boo distributor. The most prominent is Lighthouse Publishing Group, Inc., whose books boast a variety of authors—including Cook himself—and cover such topics as stock marke trading strategies, real estate investment, wealth enhancement, entity planning, and personal enrichment.

Of the some 30 Lighthouse titles currently in print, seven have been on major best-selling lists. Three have hit the *New York Times'* business book best-seller list: *Wall Street Mone Machine*, *Stock Market Miracles*, an *Business Buy the Bible*, all by Cook. The company released several new titles during 1999, including *Safety 1st Investing*. Currently under production is a new *Wall Street Money Machine* series.

Recent acquisitions on the publishing side have also spurred growth The company is continually building

ONE OF WCFC'S SECRETS TO SUCCESS IS ITS TEACHING METHODS—BASED ON A BLEND OF EXPERIENTIAL AND ROTE LEARNING—THAT MAKES ITS EDUCATIONAL PROCESS ONE OF A KIND.

s publishing business through its ublishing concerns Lighthouse ublishing Group, Inc., Worldwide ublishers, Inc., Origin Book Sellers, ıc., and Gold Leaf Press, Inc.

In addition to these publishing ɔncerns, WCFC sponsors *Explana-ons*, a newsletter that provides sub-ribers with continuing education ɔout the stock market and the com-any's trading strategies. Sales of *xplanations* increased by 244 percent om 1998 to 1999, with 1,782 and ,350 subscriptions, respectively. In ɔoo, *Explanations* plans to increase s page count, explore inclusion of utside advertisers in its circulation, ıd institute an aggressive marketing ımpaign to educate and advertise VCFC's products and services.

Roster of Services

WCFC's activities reach beyond educational seminars and printed ıaterials; the company maintains a ɔster of additional services and pro-rams that complement its primary mphases. Information Quest, Inc. Q), for example, markets the I.Q. ager™, a service that provides cus-ɔmers with up-to-date market news ıd stock quotes. IQ experienced gnificant changes in 1999, and has eared itself to increase value and performance in 2000. In addition, IQ is beta testing new information delivery technology for its pagers that will keep them on the cutting edge.

Left Coast Advertising, Inc. is a full-service advertising agency initially formed to allow WCFC to keep agency commissions in-house. Left Coast produces and places advertising in a variety of media formats, including radio, television, Internet, and newspaper and print for WCFC and its subsidiaries.

Ideal Travel Concepts, Inc. (ITC) provides travel-related services to WCFC and the public, including domestic and international airline and car rental reservations, tour packages, and cruises. ITC's Memphis office also markets travel agent packages and has more than 18,000 affiliated independent travel agents. Currently, ITC is updating its travel reservation system, establishing a user-friendly Internet site, and working on attracting top travel industry management.

Growth and Motivation

From 1994 to 1998, WCFC experienced tremendous growth; revenues alone grew from $1.9 million to $118 million. True to its mission, the company retained its position as the foremost provider of financial innovation and education in America. In 1999, the company continued that expansion as it matured and concentrated on building its infrastructure. The firm's seminar subsidiaries reported very high attendance, and the WCFC Web site was highlighted by the *Securities Trader* handbook as having the most new investment strategies.

New events and seminars are on the horizon as Wade Cook Financial Corporation continues to pursue an expanded market share for its existing products and services, while creating new products and services that complement and extend existing lines. For the company and its founder, this kind of success is very motivating.

From its myriad of services and seminars, to its newsletter, books, and Web site, WCFC has established itself at the premier financial educator in the world.

PacifiCare of Washington

GUIDED CONTINUOUSLY BY ITS VISION AN[D] VALUES, PACIFICARE OF WASHINGTON SHAPES THE MARKETPLACE FOR HEALTH CAR[E]. PACIFICARE'S VISION STATEMENT, "WE ARE AN ORGANIZATION OF DEDICATE[D] PEOPLE COMMITTED TO IMPROVING THE QUALITY OF THOSE LIVES WE TOUCH," IS A[N] ACCURATE REFLECTION OF THE WAY THE COMPANY WORKS DAILY, AS IT INTERACTS WIT[H] THE MULTIPLE STAKEHOLDERS CONCERNED WITH THE SUCCESS OF THE HEALTH CAR[E] system in Washington State. Originally established in Clark County in 1986, PacifiCare moved its headquarters to Seattle in 1995 and became a key player in the health care industry. PacifiCare pioneered a no-cost Medicare plan in the state, one of the many innovations that PacifiCare has championed to stay ahead of ever changing consumer preferences for health coverage.

One thing is certain. In a constantly evolving industry, the PacifiCare of today will not be the PacifiCare of tomorrow. The company will continue to adapt, grow, and anticipate in order to meet and beat the expectations of its customers.

Relentless Pursuit of Quality

Another innovation that PacifiCare has brought to Seattle is the city's first-ever consumer report card on quality, called the Quality Index. PacifiCare received the 1999 Paul Ellwood Award for Leadership for bringing accountability into the health care system. Responding to consumer demands for understandable information on quality and service, PacifiCare's Quality Index offers an in-depth comparison of clinical quality, service, and satisfaction among the major medical groups in the Northwest.

The Quality Index highlights PacifiCare's top-performing providers in western Washington, encouraging the sharing of the best medical and service practices among medical groups, and raising the bar on quality for the entire industry. The Quality Index reports on data that the medical groups themselves provide to PacifiCare. The company's business model has always been to collaborate with organized groups of physicians, to allow information and competition to drive improved performance and, hence, improved customer satisfaction.

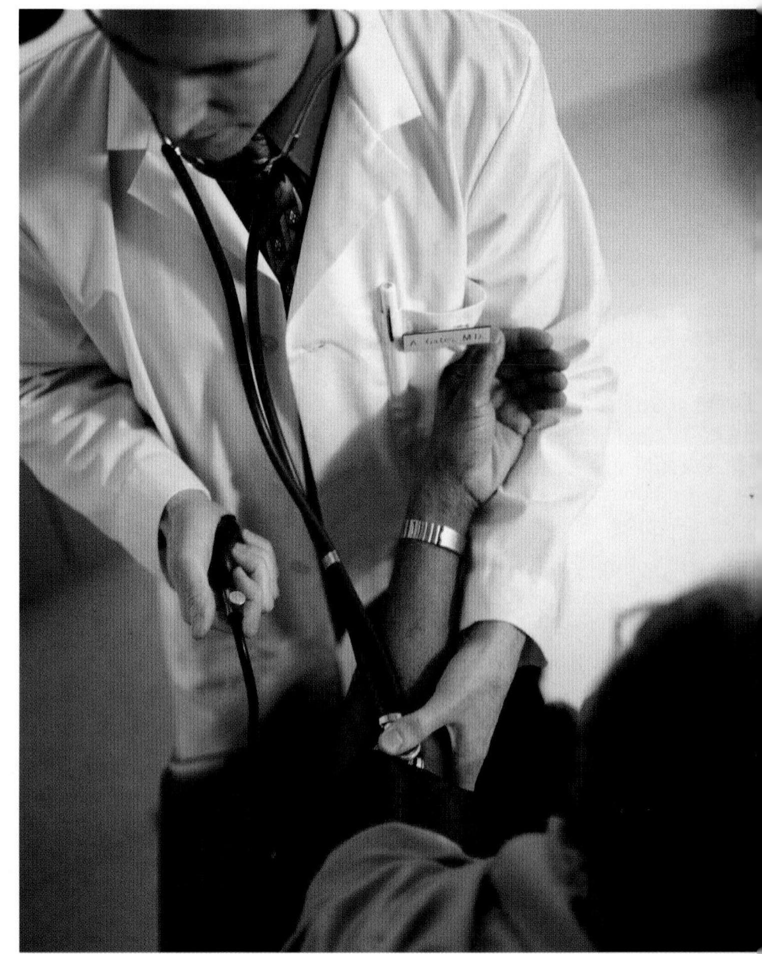

PACIFICARE OF WASHINGTON IS A MISSION-DRIVEN ORGANIZATION, DEDICATED TO IMPROVING THE HEALTH OF ITS MEMBERS AND THE SUCCESS OF ITS PROVIDER PARTNERS.

Health and Success

PacifiCare is a mission-driven organization, dedicated to improving the health of its members and the success of its provider partners. PacifiCare views its role as the facilitator of a successful relationship between the patient and the physician. As a facilitator, PacifiCare translates consumer expectations into products and services that will also assure longer-term success and stability for medical groups.

The company understands that physicians are a major voice in the community. If they aren't happy with PacifiCare, then its members aren't happy either. To ensure the success of physicians in this system, PacifiCare invests in state-of-the-art programs to help both doctors and patients manage chronic diseases such as diabetes and congestive heart failure. This kind of commitment is a cornerstone of PacifiCare's mission in action.

Getting the right care at the righ[t] time is another cornerstone, which is why PacifiCare introduced an express referrals program. Concerned with the feedback from members that it took too long to get a referra[l] to a specialist, PacifiCare worked wit[h] its contracted medical groups to allow members direct access to 16 different physician specialty types.

Listening to its members and its providers is fundamental to what PacifiCare does. Every year, the company holds town hall meetings for its members, to hear directly from them about what is working nd what isn't. Four hundred seniors ı a room can provide a lot of infor- ıation about what might improve 'acifiCare's Medicare product. The ey, though, is not just listening to s members. It's doing something bout the issues they raise. That ind of listening, combined with ocused, dedicated action, is what ıakes PacifiCare different.

ctivism

As demonstrated by its town hall meetings, PacifiCare is commit- ed to making a difference, not only o its members and physician allies, ut also within the communities it erves. PacifiCare has a charitable oundation, funded and staffed by eattle employees, that gives money o community-based organizations ocused on youth, education, and eniors. Stuffee, PacifiCare's Fit Kids ıascot and community service "vol- nteer," is a blue-haired, six-foot doll hat tours area schools and attends pecial events to teach children the alue of nutrition, exercise, and ody health.

In addition to its support of ommunity services, PacifiCare is n important contributor to political ctivism in the state. Preserving access o affordable health care is a critical nitiative for the company. Competi- ion among products and between roviders is healthy, and, by its very ature, drives higher quality and satis- action for consumers. Innovation is the nechanism through which PacifiCare s able to offer affordable health care roducts and services, and incentives, ather than mandates, are the tools 'acifiCare believes will assure con- inued choice for Washingtonians.

In the end, PacifiCare's job is to lign the incentives of the purchasers, onsumers, and providers of health are services—assuring a win-win ituation for everyone. The company's elationship with its members, its ollaboration with physicians, and ts rentless focus on quality make t uniquely positioned to succeed in loing just that. Certainly, PacifiCare ıas changed the face of health care n Washington State, and the organi- ation will continue playing a vital ole in meeting industry challenges or years to come.

Stuffee, PacifiCare's Fit Kids mascot and community service "volunteer," is a blue-haired, six-foot doll that tours area schools and attends special events to teach children the value of nutrition, exercise, and body health.

Established in Clark County in 1986, PacifiCare moved its headquarters to Seattle in 1995 and became a key player in the health care industry.

Insignia International Inc.

INSIGNIA INTERNATIONAL INC.'S UNIQU[E] OFFICE SUITE CONCEPT HELPS BUSINESSES PROJECT A PROFESSIONAL IMAGE THAT I[S] NECESSARY FOR SUCCESS IN TODAY'S BUSINESS WORLD. AN UPSCALE, COST-EFFECTIV[E] ALTERNATIVE TO A TRADITIONAL BUSINESS CENTER, INSIGNIA SUITES PROVIDE TENANT[S] WITH THEIR OWN FRONT DOOR, FULL SIGNAGE, AND UNLIMITED ACCESS TO COMMO[N] FACILITIES. IN TRADITIONAL BUSINESS CENTERS, TENANTS ARE OFTEN LOCATED IN [A] long row of cubbyholes. "Our objective is to provide affordable, first-class offices or suites with all of the bells and whistles, so our tenants have no up-front capital costs when setting up their offices," says Insignia President Ken Gordon Jr.

It's a formula that has been successful since 1990, when Gordon established Insignia's first office suites in Calgary, where the company is headquartered. Insignia is now Canada's largest provider of full-service office space, offering high-profile, innovative office solutions. The firm's growth in Seattle and Denver, as well as across the United States, is taking place at a remarkable pace.

Leasing Luxury

Insignia's bells and whistles include boardrooms for meetings of from two to 18 people, an elegantly appointed reception area, a fully stocked kitchen, photocopier, fax machine, high-speed Internet connection, and telephone system with integrated voice mail. A complimentary, fully furnished guest office is also available for clients or out-of-town personnel.

Support services are included in each Insignia tenant's lease. An Insignia receptionist answers the phone for each company, greets visitors, handles mail, and manages package delivery and pickup. Administrative and secretarial support is also available, for an additional cost, to help with word processing, database management, desktop publishing, filing, research, and assembly of promotional material. "We've been successful because we give small tenants the ability to lease in a world-class building at significant savings and with flexible leasing terms," says Gordon.

INSIGNIA INTERNATIONAL INC.'S UNIQUE OFFICE SUITE CONCEPT HELPS BUSINESSES PROJECT A PROFESSIONAL IMAGE THAT IS NECESSARY FOR SUCCESS IN TODAY'S BUSINESS WORLD.

In comparison with a conventional lease, Gordon estimates businesses can save from 30 to 50 percent by leasing under Insignia's terms. These savings can amount to thousands of dollars a month, in some cases, and tenants don't have the headaches of trying to hir[e] and supervise support staff or deal with the building management or utility companies. Tenants appreciate Insignia's flexible leasing terms. New companies can enjoy peace of mind with a short-term lease; in some cases, Insignia leases are for as little as six months, whereas most buildings managed by other companies require much longer leases. And when a tenant is ready to grow, Insignia will accommodat[e] the firm's need for additional space.

Wells Fargo Center

The 38th and 39th floors of Seattle' Wells Fargo Center—with their panoramic views—provide Insignia tenants not only top-quality office space, but also a stunning setting in which to conduct business. Considere[d] Class AAA space, the Wells Fargo Center is a unique, first-class building in the heart of the city. Insignia tenants enjoy spectacular Puget Sound and mountain views, as well as views of the San Juan Islands and commuter ferries. This setting is reflected in th[e]

▶ T. BRUSKATTER

▶ T. BRUSKATTER

AN UPSCALE, COST-EFFECTIVE ALTERNATIVE TO A TRADITIONAL BUSINESS CENTER, INSIGNIA SUITES PROVIDE TENANTS WITH THEIR OWN FRONT DOOR, FULL SIGNAGE, AND UNLIMITED ACCESS TO COMMON FACILITIES.

ophisticated interior decor of the uilding. The company's tenants an purchase their own office furniture r rent custom-designed furniture rom Insignia to complement the ecor.

The firm's tenants can also take dvantage of reciprocal arrangements vith other Insignia properties when hey travel. They can access other nsignia properties at no extra charge or a place to work, hold meetings, r obtain support services. Current nsignia locations include Seattle; Calgary; Vancouver, British Columbia; Toronto; and Denver, with plans nder way for expansion into other najor U.S. cities.

Home-based businesses not ready o invest in downtown space can enefit from Insignia's increasingly opular corporate ID program, which rovides three levels of service. The rogram starts with an ID Image eattle option, allowing an individual r a company to use the Wells Fargo ddress on their letterhead. Insignia akes care of mail handling and package receipt. At the next level, the Corporate Image option provides ersonal telephone answering services, voice mailbox, and the services in he ID Image option. Specifically esigned for the business needing a art-time office downtown, the third level, Office Image, provides a furnished office for 10 hours a week, as well as the other corporate ID services.

Varied Tenants, a Variety of Properties

A broad spectrum of businesses take advantage of Insignia's leasing space, ranging from start-up dot-coms and national software developers to legal offices, executive search firms, professional consultants, court reporters, and a number of entrepreneurial businesses.

"Lawyers especially appreciate our services," says Gordon. "The boutique law firms need first-class space, but often don't need to lease an entire floor, which most quality buildings require. With fewer support staff required, they also save substantial costs and have more time to focus on their work."

Insignia treats all of its tenants like family. A directory of tenants is published for each site, with a complete listing of the companies and contact names and a profile of what the company does. The multitenant layout and shared common facilities encourage frequent interaction between Insignia tenants. For smaller companies, these networking opportunities have often proved invaluable.

Whether a company needs a virtual office, a single office, or a multiple-office suite, Insignia provides the complete office solution that can save businesses money and time.

INCUBATED WITHIN AND THEN SPUN OU FROM MICROSOFT, AND NOW HEADQUARTERED IN BELLEVUE, WASHINGTON, EXPEDIA, INC HAS SWIFTLY EMERGED AS A LEADING PLAYER IN THE TRAVEL INDUSTRY, UTILIZING INTERNE TECHNOLOGY TO CARVE A NEW BUSINESS, AND ESTABLISHING ITSELF AS A FORCE TO B RECKONED WITH. DESPITE THE COMPANY'S TREMENDOUS GROWTH TO DATE, PRESIDENT AN CEO RICHARD BARTON STILL SEES AN EXTRAORDINARY AMOUNT OF OPPORTUNITY AHEAI

"The way I view this is really that we've taken the first 100 strides of a marathon," says Barton, Expedia's dynamic founder. "Although Expedia is a huge E-commerce player today, and the travel category is the largest commerce category on-line, it's still a tiny, tiny fraction of the travel and tourism business worldwide. We have a limitless opportunity from our perspective to continue to penetrate that business." Barton's vision has turned Expedia into a dot-com success story. In 1994, while an executive at Microsoft, Barton was handpicked by Bill Gates to investigate and build a business case for an electronic "coffee-table" product for the consumer travel market.

Barton quickly realized that a CD-ROM confined to destination reviews and information would have limited potential, but that the Internet would provide the ideal medium for the future of travel. Expedia made its Web debut in October 1996, pro viding a smorgasbord of travel infor mation and services for its customer

On November 10, 1999—the day Barton's first child was born—Expedia went on the stock market with its initial public offering (IPO) The company has since become on of the nation's top 10 travel agencie (on- or off-line), and it continues t remain at the forefront of dramatic changes in the way consumers thin about, plan for, and book travel.

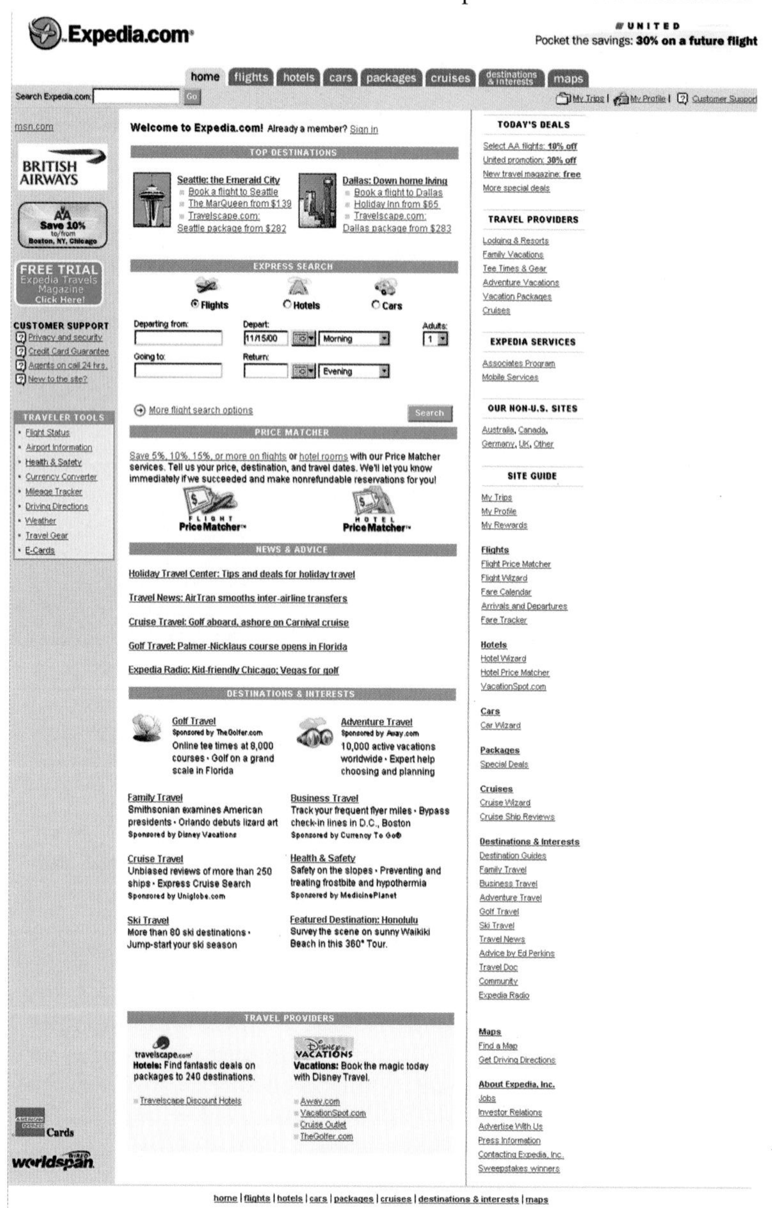

THE EXPEDIA, INC. WEB SITE, WWW.EXPEDIA.COM HELPS TRAVELERS NAVIGATE THE INCEDIBLY BROAD SET OF TRAVEL OPTIONS WITHIN SERVICES SUCH AS FLIGHT, LODGING, CAR RENTAL, PACKAGES, AND CRUISES, AND HELPS THEM OBTAIN THE TRIP THAT MEETS THEIR REQUIREMENTS.

An Emphasis on Options

The Expedia Web site, located at www.expedia.com, helps traveler navigate the incredibly broad set of travel options within services such as flight, lodging, car rental, packages, and cruises, and helps them obtain the trip that meets their requirements. The site also helps travelers support their travel decisions with copious amounts of information—visual and audio presentations about specific destinations, point-to-point maps, and other, more general information

Recognizing the diverse needs of travelers, Expedia emphasizes variety in the services it offers, providing custom ers with additional specialty travel services to address areas such as adventure vacations, family travel, cruises, gol vacations, and business travel.

The options and the ease with which customers can peruse those options have won admirers among the media and industry experts. In 2000 alone, www.expedia.com was awarded *PC Magazine's* Editors' Choice; Yahoo! Internet Life's Best Overall Travel Site; Gomez Advisors Number One Travel Site awards fo winter, spring, and summer 2000; and *PC World's* 2000 World Class Award for Best Travel Site.

Since its 1996 debut, Expedia has extended its reach with three international outposts: Canada in May 1997,

ıe United Kingdom in November
›98, and Germany in September
›99. Besides the IPO, the company
›ok giant strides forward in 1999,
eeking to establish a brand identity
nd develop stronger, more direct
elationships with its customers.

evolutionizing the Business

The company holds an enviable position in a commerce category ›oised for explosive growth. According ›o Forrester Research, on-line leisure ›ravel in the United States accounted ›or $7.8 billion of the 1999 E-commerce ›narket, compared to $6.5 billion in ›najor convenience markets such as ›oftware, books, and music. Forrester's J.S. Leisure Travel Report expects ›he travel category to reach $32 billion ›y 2004. Barton believes the company ›ill keep growing as on-line technology ›ontinues to improve.

"As bandwidth increases, and as ›he Web gets a lot faster and becomes ›medium for real interactivity, the ›ravel experience gets better and bet›er and richer and richer," Barton ›ays. "In the world of transactional ›elevision, travel is a killer applica›ion. There's clearly tremendous ›rowth potential."

Barton points out another key growth area—on-line bookings. Currently, they account for less than 1 percent of the leisure travel market, but that number is expected to change rapidly, and Expedia is seizing the opportunity.

The company's employees have firsthand knowledge of the industry they're watching. Erik Blachford, Expedia's vice president of marketing, is a former European bike guide. Richard Bangs, editor at large, is known as the pioneer of adventure travel, thanks to his rafting voyages on more than 35 of the world's rivers. Bangs also founded the world's largest adventure travel company, Mountain Travel-Sobek.

Barton, who has climbed Mount Rainier, is an adventure enthusiast in his own right. His commitment to Expedia reflects a taste for the adventure of establishing new frontiers in business.

"There are very few fundamental changes in business," Barton says. "The introduction of the Internet and ubiquitous cost-free connectivity is literally reshaping businesses. Because of that, there is an opportunity to create a global travel marketplace and truly revolutionize this business."

Expedia has swiftly emerged as a leading player in the travel industry, utilizing Internet technology to carve a new business and establishing itself as a force to be reckoned with (top).

Expedia emphasizes variety in the services it offers, providing travelers with additional specialty travel services to address areas such as adventure vacations, family travel, cruises, golf vacations, and business travel (bottom).

NIKETOWN SEATTLE GIVES NIKE INC.—ON OF THE WORLD'S LEADING SPORTS AND FITNESS COMPANIES—A PROMINENT FOOTHOLD IN CITY THAT PRIDES ITSELF ON ITS PROGRESSIVE IMAGE. THE STORE OPENED IN SEATTLE ON JUL 15, 1996, CHRISTENED BY A BEVY OF LOCAL CELEBRITIES AND SPORTS PERSONALITIES. THEN MAYOR NORM RICE APPEARED WITH REPRESENTATIVES FROM SEATTLE'S PROFESSIONAL SPORT TEAMS, INCLUDING SEATTLE MARINERS KEN GRIFFEY JR. AND JAY BUHNER. SEATTLE'S NBA franchise—the SuperSonics—and the NFL's Seahawks also participated, along with members of the Boys and Girls Clubs of King County.

Development of the NikeTown site has been one of the most visible elements of Seattle's continuing efforts to revitalize the downtown area. Located at 1500 Sixth Avenue—just six blocks from Seattle's famed Pike Place Market—the two-story NikeTown, complete with a 16-foot Nike Swoosh trademark high above the store entrance, towers over drivers entering Seattle from Interstate 5.

"NikeTown is for all athletes and the dreams they chase," says Lisa Clausen, general manager, U.S. Retail Division. "If you love sports, this is where the Nike brand and Just Do It come to life. The stores showcase Nike's rich sports heritage and innovations, while serving as valuable community resources for sports and fitness activities."

Honoring Athletes

The huge banner at the entrance to NikeTown is reserved for an image of the region's most recognizable athlete. Until his departure to the Cincinnati Reds, Griffey held that spot. For several months afterward, the banner featured only question marks, and local newspapers speculated about who would succeed the great Mariner center fielder. The answer turned out to be Gary Payton, perennial NBA All-Pro.

Customers entering the 24,000-square-foot store are treated to archival/audiovisual presentations about some of the Pacific Northwest's accomplished athletes. Besides the well-known names of Griffey and Payton, there are such luminaries as Picabo Street, women's downhill skiing champion and Olympic gold medalist. Another presentation recounts the career of Oregon's Steve Prefontaine—a great middle-distanc runner of the early 1970s, and Nike's first track-and-field athlete endorser.

More Than Just a Store

NikeTown stores are designed to showcase and build brand identity, and to provide consumers with a three-dimensional view of the company. Like other corporate-driven retail outlets, the stores give the company the means to market its footwear, apparel, and equipment lines in an atmosphere created for maximum effectiveness.

The Nike message has always combined practical utility with inspiration. The company takes its name from the winged Greek goddes

DEVELOPMENT OF THE NIKETOWN SITE HAS BEEN ONE OF THE MOST VISIBLE ELEMENTS OF SEATTLE'S CONTINUING EFFORTS TO REVITALIZE THE DOWNTOWN AREA.

victory, who awarded wreaths to e victors of battles or contests.

In keeping with that spirit, the ikeTown store moves beyond stanrd retail models to create an arena information about Nike products, well as inspiration for the aspiring hlete. For active members of the cal athletic community, the store also a central meeting point for ose who want to get involved in assroots sports clubs, events, and nics.

The store interior uses motifs remiscent of a Roman coliseum or stadin, but these themes are more than pretty frame. NikeTown features a mplete lineup of Nike sports footear, apparel, and equipment in a otivationally driven retail environent. NikeTown is also home to st-rate customer care and the best ailable Nike product knowledge.

The stores also provide the comny with valuable testing grounds r new retail ideas, as well as direct stomer feedback on products, serces, and displays. And while all ikeTowns share a number of key ysical elements, company leaders courage each store to develop a stinct personality.

"We want to encourage people at ikeTown to participate in sports creating an engaging environment at really gets across the unique rsonality and philosophy of Nike as a sports company," says John Hoke, design creative director. "By combining Nike's product innovation with the excitement of the sports world, NikeTown creates a powerful and engaging shopping experience."

The Nike message has always combined practical utility with inspiration. The company takes its name from the winged Greek goddess of victory, who awarded wreaths to the victors of battles or contests.

Respecting Diversity

The first NikeTown opened in Portland, Oregon, in 1990, and parent company Nike Inc. is headquartered in Beaverton, a Portland suburb. The company markets its products in more than 100 countries and prides itself on a progressive approach to business, including support for environmental causes and a strong diversity agenda.

For example, according to statistics from national gay and lesbian rights organizations, Nike is one of only 87 companies among the Fortune 500 who extend benefit coverage to employees' same-sex permanent partners. "Nike considers its leadership in this area to be a competitive advantage," says Jeffrey Cava, vice president, human resources. "By expanding our support for all employees and their families, we're putting specific actions behind our commitment to a diverse workplace."

NikeTown features a complete lineup of Nike sports footwear, apparel, and equipment in a motivationally driven retail environment. NikeTown is also home to first-rate customer care and the best available Nike product knowledge.

IN A MARKET DEVOID OF ANY LOCA PUBLICATION FOCUSING SPECIFICALLY ON THE HOME, *Seattle Homes and Lifestyles* MAGAZIN CREATED A NICHE WHERE IT HAS MANAGED TO THRIVE. THE MAGAZINE WA ESTABLISHED IN 1996 BY ITS PARENT COMPANY, WIESNER PUBLISHING, LLC, WHIC OPERATES SISTER HOMES AND LIFESTYLES PUBLICATIONS IN COLORADO, ST. LOUIS, AN ATLANTA. ● WITH A CIRCULATION OF 30,000, *Seattle Homes and Lifestyles* HA established itself as a trusted local resource. Current newsstand distribution is approximately 15,000, with sales consistently outperforming all local and many national magazine titles. The subscriber list, now about 8,300 in number, grows each day. Remaining issues are included in executive relocation packages for large corporations and are distributed at key local events.

Editorial Focus and Content

Serving as the lifestyle diary and guidebook for home owners in the Puget Sound region, *Seattle Homes and Lifestyles* seeks to entertain, inspire, and inform its readers by showcasing the finest homes and landscapes in the area. By revealing the personalities behind the projects, exploring the decisions that are made, and providing useful information, the magazine hopes to give readers the resources and insight they need to beautify their own surroundings.

The magazine is published seven times a year. Regular features include interiors and landscapes of the region's hottest homes; glimpses into the intriguing lifestyles of celebrities and other area residents; design trends and arresting architecture; innovative home ideas, services, and products; a month-by-month gardening calendar; local artisans; culinary delights and hands-on recipes; and features on travel, entertaining, and wine.

Editor Fred Albert has piloted *Seattle Homes and Lifestyles* magazine since its inception. Prior to that time, he spent more than a decade covering home design for *The Seattle Times*, and served as a contributing editor for *Seattle* and *Pacific Northwest* magazines, covering home design for both publications. Albert is the author of *Barkitecture*, published by Abbeville Press, and is coauthor of *American Design: The Northwest*, a coffee-table book published by Bantam. His writing has also been featured in numerous national and internationa publications, including *Home, America HomeStyle & Gardening, Landscape Design, Hauser*, and *Romantic Homes*. A graduate of Yale University, Albe has made frequent appearances on radio and television programs, includin ABC's *Good Morning America*.

Highlighting Seattle's Specialties

The magazine's flavor is distinctly local. Issues have featured house boats on Lake Union, mansions in Redmond, cottages in the San Juans and gardens in West Seattle. For Publisher Pat Kelly, this diversity is a reminder of the good fortune are residents share.

In a recent issue, Kelly published a teasing admonishment reminding

READERS OF *SEATTLE HOMES AND LIFESTYLES* CAN CHECK THE MONTHLY GARDEN PLANNER FOR TIPS, CLASSES, AND SALES, AND CAN ENJOY STUNNING PHOTOS OF THE REGION'S TOP GARDENS (RIGHT).

EVERY ISSUE OF *SEATTLE HOMES AND LIFESTYLES* IS PACKED WITH DECORATION AND REMODELING IDEAS (LEFT).

STEVEN YOUNG

▲ SEATTLE HOMES AND LIFESTYLES

eaders that they live in one of merica's truly pristine areas, yet equently overlook their good fortune ecause of day-to-day obligations. We've gotten too busy," she wrote. We've stopped enjoying the very hings that make Seattle such a popu- ır vacation destination. For instance, vhen was the last time you were on a erry or walked through Pike Place Aarket and watched them throw ish? I think it's time to be a tourist gain in my city."

Kelly hails from Miami. After pending nine years at *The Miami Herald* in the newspaper's advertising department, she decided to leave for a one-year stint working for the United Nations as an editor in Sudan and Kenya. Returning from abroad, she joined the staff of *The Denver Post.* In 1993, Kelly joined Wiesner Publishing as the publisher of *Colorado Homes and Lifestyles* magazine, increasing profits by more than 500 percent. She led the start-up effort for *Seattle Homes and Lifestyles* in 1996, hiring and training an entire magazine staff.

Wiesner has emerged as the largest publisher of regional homes and lifestyles titles in the nation. E. Patrick Wiesner, founder of the publishing house, continues to stress publishing fundamentals: a combination of editorial integrity and common business sense. "We have a solid company," Wiesner says. "We're making money, and we have good magazines, good management, and outstanding people."

Solid management, staff, and editorial direction have proved to be *Seattle Homes and Lifestyles'* keys to initial success, and will surely enable it to endure over time. Both the readership and the community truly benefit from the magazine's unique contribution.

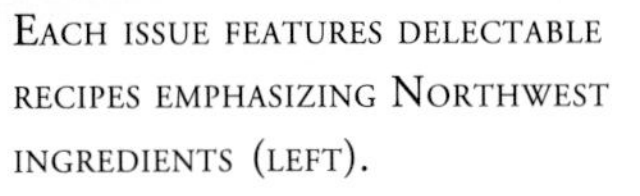

Each issue features delectable recipes emphasizing Northwest ingredients (left).

Seattle Homes and Lifestyles is available on newsstands throughout the Puget Sound region (right).

▲ GREGG KROGSTAD

The magazine highlights outstanding artisans and personalities who make the Northwest special (left).

Seattle Homes and Lifestyles features work by the region's top architects, showing readers how to plan the home of their dreams (right).

Activate Corporation is a specialize digital media infrastructure services company and one of the top servic providers and producers of live Internet events. Since Activate's inceptio in 1997, the company has focused on providing complete, end-to-end solution for businesses that want to broadcast audio and video content to Interne and intranet audiences. Activate's motto—Your audio. Your video. Directl to your audience.—reflects the company's commitment to providing complete solutions and support to help businesses communicate their message to a specific audience. With Webcasting, businesses are able to transform a one-way message into a one-to-many communication, reaching an audience anytime, anyplace in the world via the Internet or corporate intranets.

Activate provides customers with the necessary tools to deploy and integrate streaming media capabilities into their existing business models. The company's services include event Webcasting; live, 24-hour, seven-day-a-week streaming for radio, television, and Internet-only programming; rich media advertising; and on-demand Webcasting of audio and video content. Activate helps companies use streaming media as a business tool, including corporate communications, training seminars, and customer support.

Digital media is one of the fastest-growing segments of the Internet services market. More and more companies are looking to enrich their communications with business and consumer audiences by applying digital media content to their Web sites. FBR RichMedia Research estimates the total market for digital media will grow to $8 billion in 2004.

Today, streaming media is targeted primarily to desktop computers or equivalent devices with Internet access. Over the next few years, the range of possible devices and destinations for digital media will explode, expanding to technologies such as handheld wireless devices. Activate is unique in the breadth and scope of its Webcasting tools, and continues to be on the forefront of the streaming media industry.

Activate Corporation's motto—Your audio. Your video. Directly to your audience.—reflects the company's commitment to providing complete solutions and support to help businesses communicate their message to a specific audience.

Building Momentum and a Future

From software development and telephony to Internet and professional services, Activate leverages the experience of its seasoned management team to direct its bright future. The team brings more than 125 years of experience collectively from companies such as Microsoft, RealNetworks, AT&T, Lucent, Amazon.com, Mercata, Atrieva, and ONSALE, Inc.

Jeff Schrock, Activate cofounder and chief executive officer, is responsible for the vision, overall management, and leadership of the company Through his leadership, the firm ha grown to be the foremost provider of streaming media for businesses worldwide. Schrock has also served as a management consultant in the areas of product marketing and development strategies for Microsoft, Digital, and Compaq.

Chris Maskill, cofounder and senior vice president of business development, is responsible for business development and daily executive-level involvement in various aspects of the business. Under his leadership, Activate generated more than $1 million in revenues during its first 16 months of operation. Maskill's experience in Internet media includes several years with RealNetworks and AT&T Network Services.

The Activate team expanded with the addition of Stewart Chapin, Garr Welch, and Jon Brown, who collectively brought more than 60 years of experience in the telecommunications and high-tech industries. Chapin—who held the position of vice president of product development at AT&T Wireless Communications, where he managed the nationwide launch of AT&T's Digital PCS service—has responsibility for the marketing product management, and communications components of Activate's business. Welch, responsible for les and field operations for Activate, ings more than 25 years of experience om McCaw Cellular, AT&T, and ucent Technologies. And Brown, as ctivate's vice president of engineer- g, manages the core development Activate's business—its network d system architecture—as well as aluating future technologies.

In the spring of 2000, Activate pointed Dennis Shepard, formerly th Mercata, as chief operating officer. e brings more than 30 years of op- ational experience to his role Activate. The company's highly perienced and knowledgeable ex- utive team looks forward to leading ctivate into the 21st century as the ading digital media services company.

Building with History, a Company th Purpose

Activate occupied its Seattle head- quarters in November 1999, giving e company's world-class team of oadcast operations, engineering, d business professionals their first pportunity to work and play together nder one roof. By converting the storic, 60,000-square-foot, former rment factory into a state-of-the-art gital media broadcast operations nter, Activate has provided its em- oyees with the necessary resources to serve customers with the highest-quality streaming media.

The rooftop hosts Activate's satellite downlink facility, with 15 dishes providing up to 60 channels of simultaneous downlink capacity. Activate's team manages the capture, encoding, and publishing of thousands of media clips each month for hundreds of customers, and has developed specialized applications that range from reservations systems for live events to real-time, Web-based reporting tools that provide Activate with a competitive advantage. In addition, Activate has secondary production and operations capabilities in New York and Toronto, and has sales offices in Boston, Los Angeles, and Chicago.

Just the Beginning

At Activate, employees are key to the success of the business. A diverse group with talents from high-tech and broadcast companies, Activate's employees bring considerable experience in rich media production. Professional experience is only part of what makes the Activate team a success. Encouraged to play as hard as they work, Activate's pet-friendly office features a second-floor basketball court, and combines laughter with intensity and focus. Bringing together an assortment of unique and talented individuals, Activate's team includes a national fiddle champion, sailors, stand-up comedians, mountain climbers, and triathletes.

Activate combines experience and passion to provide the highest-quality streaming media services for businesses today. Perhaps that is the reason Activate is among today's top five service providers delivering digital media content over the Internet.

Activate's seasoned management team includes (standing), Jon Brown, Jeff Schrock, Dennis Shepard, (kneeling), Gary Welch, Stew Chapin, Chris maskill.

Activate occupied its Seattle headquarters in November 1999, giving the company's world-class team of broadcast operations, engineering, and business professionals their first opportunity to work and play together under one roof.

Making its debut in 1997 as the firs privately owned casino in the history of Washington State, Freddie's Club Casin in Renton is today one of the state's busiest and most famous nontribal casino. Despite some initial public skepticism, the casino has exceeded the most libera estimates of how well it would be received, and today fills the area's demand fo smaller casinos with clean, tasteful ambience and mainstream accessibility.

The story of Freddie's begins with its founder and principal owner, Fred Steiner, a gaming entrepreneur with three decades of experience in the state of Washington. His career began inauspiciously: Steiner, a 1962 graduate of Renton High School, was a pinsetter at a bowling alley that once sat where his casino stands today.

Steiner's father, Joseph, was a trendsetter in his own way, establishing Renton's first drive-in restaurant, known appropriately enough as Joe's. With money saved from odd jobs, Fred Steiner purchased his first business—one of his father's restaurants.

Steiner's odyssey into the gaming industry began in 1973, the year public card room gaming was introduced in Washington. He opened a three-table poker room in a Renton tavern. Three years later, Steiner took another step, selling his tavern/card room and purchasing a well-located restaurant and lounge, with the intention of adding poker. Diamond Lil's Poker Club on Rainier Avenue quickly became—and remains today—one of the most successful businesses of its kind in the Evergreen State.

Since its debut in 1997, Freddie's Club Casino has become one of Washington State's busiest, exceeding the most liberal estimates of how well it would be received.

In 1997, Steiner, along with several other poker room owners, lobbied successfully for a bill in the state legislature that allowed for nontribal gaming. The bill received nearly unanimous support, and opened tl door for privately owned table casinc in the state.

Steiner was the first to take advan tage of this historic opportunity, an Freddie's Club was born. For Steiner the keys to success were simple and straightforward: friendly dealers wh could build a rapport with the public and personalized service for customers He also wanted a congenial atmosphere, combining a sense of intimac with spaciousness.

The tangible result of Steiner's vision is on display at the Renton club, where rich oak paneling and wainscoting create a leisurely yet luxu rious atmosphere. The well-appointe bar and large restaurant welcome cus tomers, and let them know the club a place for relaxation and conversation, as well as gaming. The finishir touches to the atmosphere of the casino include beveled mirrors, mor

The most famous nontribal casino in the region, Freddie's Club has a luxurious, relaxing atmosphere, perfect for both conversation and gaming.

han 100 feet of brass railings, tiled vindowsills, and artwork depicting ports stars, famous entertainers, and as Vegas locales. But above all, the lub's staff works diligently to ensure hat patrons' needs are met.

Since this first casino opened, the reddie's franchise has expanded to ocations in the cities of Auburn, verett, and Fife. The Auburn location, opened in 1998, continued the radition of quality established in enton. Built with fun and extravaance in mind, the Auburn casino, vhich is larger than the Renton location, includes all the pleasures of the riginal facility, along with additions uch as the Steiner Diner, a 1950s-tyle restaurant with an authentic oda fountain, stainless steel kitchen anels, and neon signage.

In 1997, Fred Steiner, along with several other poker room owners, lobbied successfully for a bill in the state legislature that allowed for nontribal gaming. The bill received nearly unanimous support, and opened the door for privately owned table casinos in the state.

Leader in the Industry nd the Community

The success of Freddie's Club has spawned many would-be imitators. Since Freddie's Club premiered, hrongs of businessmen have sought o duplicate the many elements that nake our casino unparalleled in the narketplace," says Casino Manager Cory Thompson. "When we opened, lot of prospective casino owners and nanagers made continuous reconoitering tours. Many of them were riends of Fred Steiner—some had lobbied for the legislation that made this business possible. As our first year passed, I discovered that our name had become synonymous with a smaller casino with class and friendliness. People kept saying to me, 'I want to open a Freddie's.' I am truly proud of what we have accomplished with our first casino effort."

Drawing an estimated 2,000 patrons to its gaming tables each day, the casino has also given a lift to the surrounding area, serving as a magnet for other businesses. In Renton, where a citywide marketing effort has driven new development and attracted new business, Freddie's is a surprising player in a downtown renaissance.

Sadly, Fred Steiner died in the fall of 2000 at the age of 56. "However, the values he instilled in those he employed still live on. May Freddie rest in peace," says Thompson. And despite the continued growth of the clubs, the focus will always remain on Steiner's original goal. Each detail reflects his simple philosophy: "I want everything to be right."

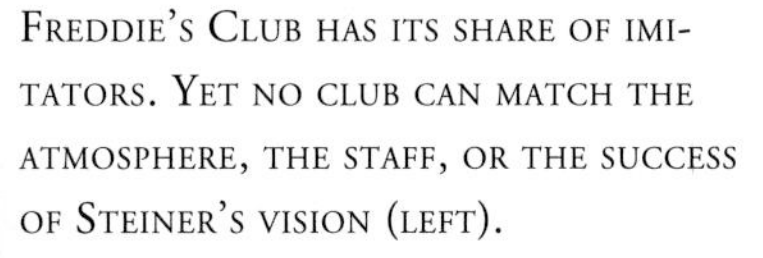

Freddie's Club has its share of imitators. Yet no club can match the atmosphere, the staff, or the success of Steiner's vision (left).

For Steiner, the keys to success were simple and straightforward: friendly dealers who could build a rapport with the public, and personalized service for customers (right).

Ask what the W in Seattle's W Hote[l] stands for, and everyone seems to have a different answer: warm, witty, won[-]derful, and whimsical are some of the most common responses. But, accordin[g] to General Manager Tom Limberg, all these words and more are wrapped up i[n] the W name, and are ultimately reflected in the hotel's service philosoph[y:] Whatever You Want, Whenever You Want It. ● The 426-room W Seattl[e,] owned and managed by Starwood Hotels & Resorts Worldwide, Inc., combines a unique union of style and substance with top-of-the-line business technology and amenities. Built for $90 million, it is the first newly constructed hotel with more than 250 rooms in downtown Seattle since 1983. Seattle designers Callison Architecture collaborated with Starwood representatives to establish the hotel's distinctive look and feel.

The 26-floor W Seattle features several exterior details that embody a contemporary interpretation of Seattle's classic architecture. The building is crowned by a steel and mesh pyramid, which glows softly at night and remains visible throughout downtown. With its fluted columns, capitals, cornices, and arched entries, the W building complements the historic, classical-style buildings that surround it.

◀ CALLISON ARCHITECTURE

The pyramid atop the 26-floor W Hotel shines like a beacon above downtown Seattle (top).

Each of the hotel's deluxe guest rooms features a luxurious W bed, 27-inch television, and snack and beverage bar, as well as other amenities to make a guest's stay memorable (bottom).

A Home Away from Home

The hotel's deluxe guest rooms feature the luxurious W beds, complete with 250-thread-count linens as well as goose down comforters and pillows. "Absolutely the most comfortable bed in the industry," Limberg says. Each room also features a 27-inch, color television, which includes Internet access and the option of setting up personal, secure E-mail addresses during a hotel stay. Ready when munchies strike, the snack and beverage bar is stocked with everything from traditional items to wax lips, Pez candy dispensers, and high-end microbrew beers. Other features include custom-made game boards and a state-of-the-art fitness center.

In addition, 18 percent of the W's rooms are designated as W Home Office rooms, which include extra amenities such as a combination printer/copier/fax/scanner. "Today's business traveler has a unique set of needs and expectations," Limberg says. "Seattle, as an international trade and high-tech center, is host to countless business and entertainmen[t] industry visitors each year. These individuals cannot afford to step away from mission-critical business operations back at the office. W Seattle allows these guests to stay connected to their business through a high-speed technology framework, while pampering them with hip ambience, high-quality services, and exceptional dining."

More Than Just a Good Night's Rest

Located in the very heart of downtown Seattle's financial, retail, and entertainment district, the W Hotel is just five blocks from Pike

CALLISON ARCHITECTURE

CALLISON ARCHITECTURE

From left:
The concierge will help guests with "whatever you want whenever you want it."

With seating for 120 patrons, Earth & Ocean is a unique dining experience, as well as a winner of *Food & Wine's* Best New Wine Lists.

The W Bar is a hot spot for locals, guests, and celebrities.

'lace Market and two blocks from ıe new Benaroya Symphony Hall. 'he hotel's sleek, modern, two-story ›bby, showcasing floor-to-ceiling ʼindows, is known simply as the ,iving Room—a focal point for uests to socialize, dine, drink, or imply relax.

The use of contrasting woods and treamlined furniture and fabrics is lso the focus for the W Cafe and Newsstand, a unique concept that lls a variety of needs from morning hrough night. Guests starting out heir day can grab a quick bite and 'esh juice on the run. In the evening, he space converts into a hip bar.

Recognizing Seattle's reputation s one of the country's hot spots for reat food and wine, W Seattle has artnered with Drew Nieporent— ne of America's most respected and elebrated restaurateurs, and president f the Myriad Restaurant Group— o develop the hotel's restaurant, Earth & Ocean. The restaurant's ntrance floor is finished in one-inch iles in a multicolored palette of maize, lack, leaf green, tomato, navy, and white. With seating for 120 patrons, Earth & Ocean offers a unique dining experience, led by Executive Chef Johnathan Sundstrom, who as developed an inventive lineup of nique dishes from the indigenous ounty of the Pacific Northwest.

The W Hotel is also an important enter for business meetings and conentions. Of the hotel's 336,650 quare feet of space, 10,000 square eet is dedicated to meeting and anquet areas, including nine conference rooms with floor-to-ceiling windows. An 1,800-square-foot foyer leads to a 4,500-square-foot ballroom, also adorned with floor-to-ceiling windows.

A Sign of Things to Come

The W Hotel in Seattle is one of 19 new W properties to be launched nationally and internationally through 2002—part of an industrywide boom in boutique hotels. According to Limberg, W is the fastest-growing luxury brand in the world, in part because more established hotels are still mired in the past, failing to adjust to the changing demographics of business travelers. "Our concept is a little more relaxed, a little more comfortable, a little more engaging on a one-to-one level," says Limberg. "We hope to be the social center of the city. Seattle was chosen as a target market for this concept because of its reputation as a cutting-edge city, a place for the avant-garde, and a trendsetter nationally in everything from music to coffee to customer service to technology," says Limberg. "Younger business owners and executives want a fresher experience, which W aims to provide."

CALLISON ARCHITECTURE

The hotel provides guests with a sleek, modern, two-story lobby, known as the Living Room, for dining, socializing, or simply relaxing.

BEGINNING AS A SMALL PUBLISHER OF LOCA NEWSPAPERS IN THE 1930S, TOWERY PUBLISHING, INC. TODAY PRODUCES A WIDE RANGE O COMMUNITY-ORIENTED MATERIALS, INCLUDING BOOKS (URBAN TAPESTRY SERIES), BUSINES DIRECTORIES, MAGAZINES, AND INTERNET PUBLICATIONS. BUILDING ON ITS LONG HERITAGE O EXCELLENCE, THE COMPANY HAS BECOME GLOBAL IN SCOPE, WITH CITIES FROM SAN DIEGO T SYDNEY REPRESENTED BY TOWERY PRODUCTS. IN ALL ITS ENDEAVORS, THIS MEMPHIS-BASE company strives to be synonymous with service, utility, and quality.

A Diversity of Community-Based Products

Over the years, Towery has become the largest producer of published materials for North American chambers of commerce. From membership directories that enhance business-to-business communication to visitor and relocation guides tailored to reflect the unique qualities of the communities they cover, the company's chamber-oriented materials offer comprehensive information on dozens of topics, including housing, education, leisure activities, health care, and local government.

In 1998, the company acquired Cincinnati-based Target Marketing, an established provider of detailed city street maps to more than 200 chambers of commerce throughout the United States and Canada. Now a division of Towery, Target offers full-color maps that include local landmarks and points of interest, such as recreational parks, shopping centers, golf courses, schools, industrial parks, city and county limits, subdivision names, public buildings, and even block numbers on most streets.

In 1990, Towery launched the Urban Tapestry Series, an award-winning collection of oversized, hardbound photojournals detailing the people, history, culture, environment, and commerce of various metropolitan areas. These coffee-table books highlight a community through three basic elements: an introductory essay by a noted local individual, an exquisite collection of four-color photographs, and profiles of the companies and organizations that animate the area's business life.

To date, more than 80 Urban Tapestry Series editions have been published in cities around the world from New York to Vancouver to Sydney. Authors of the books' introductory essays include former U.S. President Gerald Ford (Grand Rapids), former Alberta Premier Peter Lougheed (Calgary), CBS anchor Dar Rather (Austin), ABC anchor Hugl Downs (Phoenix), best-selling mystery author Robert B. Parker (Boston), American Movie Classics host Nick Clooney (Cincinnati), Senato Richard Lugar (Indianapolis), and Challenger Center founder June Scobee Rodgers (Chattanooga).

To maintain hands-on quality ir all of its periodicals and books, Towery has long used the latest production methods available. The company wa the first production environment in the United States to combine desktop publishing with color separations and image scanning to produce finished film suitable for burning plates for four-color printing. Today, Towery relies on state-of-the-art digital prepres services to produce more than 8,00 pages each year, containing well over 30,000 high-quality color images.

An Internet Pioneer

By combining its long-standing expertise in community-oriente published materials with advanced production capabilities, a global sales force, and extensive data managemen capabilities, Towery has emerged as a significant provider of Internet-based city information. In keeping with it overall focus on community resources the company's Internet efforts represent a natural step in the evolution of the business.

The primary product lines within the Internet division are the introCity sites. Towery's introCity sites introduce newcomers, visitors, and long-time residents to every facet of a

STEVE DAVIS

TOWERY PUBLISHING PRESIDENT AND CEO J. ROBERT TOWERY HAS EXPANDED THE BUSINESS HIS PARENTS STARTED IN THE 1930S TO INCLUDE A GROWING ARRAY OF TRADITIONAL AND ELECTRONIC PUBLISHED MATERIALS, AS WELL AS INTERNET AND MULTIMEDIA SERVICES, THAT ARE MARKETED LOCALLY, NATIONALLY, AND INTERNATIONALLY.

articular community, while simul-
neously placing the local chamber of
ommerce at the forefront of the city's
nternet activity. The sites include
ewcomer information, calendars,
hotos, citywide business listings
ith everything from nightlife to
hopping to family fun, and on-line
aps pinpointing the exact location
f businesses, schools, attractions,
nd much more.

Decades of Publishing Expertise

In 1972, current President and CEO J. Robert Towery succeeded his parents in managing the printing and publishing business they had founded nearly four decades earlier. Soon thereafter, he expanded the scope of the company's published materials to include *Memphis* magazine and other successful regional and national publications. In 1985, after selling its locally focused assets, Towery began the trajectory on which it continues today, creating community-oriented materials that are often produced in conjunction with chambers of commerce and other business organizations.

Despite the decades of change, Towery himself follows a long-standing family philosophy of unmatched service and unflinching quality. That approach extends throughout the entire organization to include more than 120 employees at the Memphis headquarters, another 80 located in Northern Kentucky outside Cincinnati, and more than 40 sales, marketing, and editorial staff traveling to and working in a growing list of client cities. All of its products, and more information about the company, are featured on the Internet at www.towery.com.

In summing up his company's steady growth, Towery restates the essential formula that has driven the business since its first pages were published: "The creative energies of our staff drive us toward innovation and invention. Our people make the highest possible demands on themselves, so I know that our future is secure if the ingredients for success remain a focus on service and quality."

Towery Publishing was the first production environment in the United States to combine desktop publishing with color separations and image scanning to produce finished film suitable for burning plates for four-color printing. Today, the company's state-of-the-art network of Macintosh and Windows workstations allows it to produce more than 8,000 pages each year, containing more than 30,000 high-quality color images.

The Towery family's publishing roots can be traced to 1935, when R.W. Towery (far left) began producing a series of community histories in Tennessee, Mississippi, and Texas. Throughout the company's history, the founding family has consistently exhibited a commitment to clarity, precision, innovation, and vision.

© JIM CORWIN

Library of Congress Cataloging-in-Publication Data

Lacitis, Erik, 1949-
Seattle : the time has come / by Erik Lacitis ; art direction by Bob Kimball.
p. cm — (Urban tapestry series)
Includes index.
ISBN 1-881096-84-X (alk. paper)
1. Seattle (Wash.)—Civilization. 2. Business enterprises—Washington (State)—Seattle.
3. Seattle (Wash.)—Economic conditions. 4. Seattle (Wash.)—Pictorial works. I. Title II.
Series

F899.S45 L33 2001
979.7'772'00222—dc21

00-066327

Towery Publishing, Inc.
The Towery Building
1835 Union Avenue
Memphis, TN 38104
www.towery.com

Printed in China.

Publisher: J. Robert Towery Executive Publisher: Jenny McDowell National Sales Manager: Stephen Hung Marketing Director: Carol Culpepper Project Directors: Andrea Glazier, Carter Gregg, Paul Lawrence, Simone Williams Executive Editor: David B. Dawson Managing Editor: Lynn Conlee Senior Editors: Carlisle Hacker, Brian L. Johnston Editors: Rebecca E. Farabough, Danna M. Greenfield, Ginny Reeves, Sabrina Schroeder Editor/Caption Writer: Stephen M. Deusner Editor/Profile Manager: Jay Adkins Profile Writer: Sean Robinson Creative Director: Brian Groppe Photography Editor: Jonathan Postal Photographic Consultant: Jim Bates Profile Designers: Rebekah Barnhardt, Laurie Beck, Glen Marshall Production Manager: Brenda Pattat Photography Coordinator: Robin Lankford Production Assistants: Robert Barnett, Loretta Lane, Robert Parrish Digital Color Supervisor: Darin Ipema Digital Color Technicians: Eric Friedl, Brent Salazar, Mark Svetz Digital Scanning Technicians: Zac Ives, Brad Long Production Resources Manager: Dave Dunlap Jr. Print Coordinator: Beverly Timmons

Photographers

▲ © ALAN BERNER / SEATTLE TIMES

Originally headquartered in London, **Allsport** has expanded to include offices in New York and Los Angeles. It pictures have appeared in every major publication in the world, and the best of its portfolio has been displayed at elite photographic exhibitions at the Royal Photographic Society and the Olympic Museum in Lausanne.

Specializing in natural-light images of the Pacific Northwest and other travel destinations, **Susan Alworth** has had her work published in *WHERE Magazine Seattle* and has photographed for Impact Photographics, Guest Informant, Crabtree Publishing, the Seattle-King County Convention and Visitors Bureau, and Vernon Publications.

As a freelance photographer, **Ellen M. Banner** has contributed news-related images to the *Seattle Times*. Originally from Camarillo, California, she specializes in photojournalism and commercial photography.

With awards from such groups as the National Press Photographers Association, **Jim Bates** specializes in news and sports photography. Originally from the Seattle area, he now works for the *Seattle Times*.

Benjamin Benschneider specializes in people profiles, nature, and architecture photography and works for the *Seattle Times*.

A four-time winner of the National Press Photographers Association Regional Photographer of the Year award, **Alan Berner** works for the *Seattle Times* as a photojournalist.

Jan Butchofsky-Houser specializes in travel photography and has coauthored the third edition of a travel guidebook, *Hidden Mexico*. Her photos have appeared in dozens of magazines, newspapers, books, advertisements, and brochures, as well as on video and album covers. She has served as an editorial/research associate for the Berkeley, California-based Ulysses Press and currently manages Dave G. Houser Stock Photography. Her awards include the Bronze Portfolio award in the Society of American Travel Writers (SATW) Photo Showcase, and a Bronze award ı the Natural Scenic category of the ATW Photo Showcase.

fter working for 12 years at Seattle-rea photo labs, **Jim Corwin** opened is own business in 1990. Originally om Portland, Oregon, he specializes ı travel, nature, people, and sports hotography, and his work has been eatured in such publications as *lational Geographic Traveler* and *usiness Week*.

s the national president of the Amer-an Society of Picture Professionals ASPP), **Danita Dellmont** specializes in nages garnered from worldwide travel.

or more than 12 years, **Terry Donnelly** f Donnelly-Austin Photography has ad images used by leading clients in ne calendar, book, and advertising gency businesses. He publishes eight nnual calendar titles that feature Donnelly-Austin images.

s the owner of Scott Eklund Photog-aphy and a regular freelance contribu-or to the *Seattle Post-Intelligencer*, **cott Eklund** specializes in editorial hotography, particularly people, oorts, and portraits. He has received wards from numerous organizations, ıch as the National Press Photogra-hers Association and Professional hotographers of America, and his lients include *National Geographic* nd *Vanity Fair*.

ee Foster, a veteran travel writer and hotographer, has had his work pub-shed in major travel magazines and ewspapers. He maintains a stock li-rary that features images of more an 250 destinations worldwide.

ireg Gilbert is the first photographer o transmit a digital photograph from jetliner while traveling across the tlantic Ocean. He specializes in eople, sports, portrait, and action hotography for the *Seattle Times*.

laving traveled throughout Africa, atin America, Europe, and the Jnited States, **Beryl Goldberg** spe-ializes in environmental, portrait, ravel, and multicultural images. As he owner of Beryl Goldberg Photog-aphy, she has had her work pub-shed in magazines and newspapers, nd for international organizations nd travel companies.

A contributing editor to *Vacations* and *Cruises & Tours* magazines and co-author of the travel guidebook *Hidden Coast of California*, **Dave G. Houser** specializes in cruise/luxury travel, personality, health, and history photography. He was the runner-up for the Lowell Thomas Travel Journalist of the Year award and was named the 1984 Society of American Travel Writers' Photographer of the Year.

With photographs in *Time*, *Newsday*, and other publications, **Thomas James Hurst** has received several awards, and he placed in the top three in the 1997 and 1999 World Press Photo competitions. He currently works for the *Seattle Times* and specializes in world conflict photography.

Specializing in still life, product, and industrial/corporate photography for his employer, Strode Photographers, **Tim J. Johnson** has a client list that includes the Frank Russell Company, Jet Tools, and Occidental Chemical Corporation.

Formerly an employee for Scripps Howard News Service in Washington, D.C., **Daniel Kim** now works for the *Seattle Times* and specializes in photojournalism. His awards include the Asian American Journalists Association Scholarship for 1999 and 2000.

After studying art in his native Ireland, **James Lemass** moved to Cambridge, Massachusetts, in 1987. His specialties include people and travel photography, and his photographs have appeared in numerous Towery publications.

Jimi Lott is a news photographer for the *Seattle Times*.

Specializing in documentary photography for the Spanish community, as well as in commercial and digital imagery, **Hugo C. Ludeña** owns Hugo-Fotografía and has done freelance work for King County Health Department. He has contributed to *La Voz*, *Latino Northwest Magazine*, and other publications.

As a principal partner and lead photographer for Strode-McGowan Photography, **Kevin McGowan** specializes in industrial, corporate, and architectural photographic assignments. He has received numerous awards and trophies from the Professional Photographers of America and the Professional Photographers of Washington.

Ray Meuse, the owner of Ray Meuse Photography, is currently working to photograph every square mile of Seattle, to produce some 1,000 archivally processed and stored prints that will show future generations how Seattle looked at the turn of the millennium. Originally from Boston, he received a photography fellowship from the National Endowment for the Arts in 1975 and served five years on the King County Arts Commission in the 1970s.

Pedro Perez specializes in marine photography, particularly fishing and boating. Originally from Five Points, California, he currently works for the *Seattle Times*.

Greg Probst joined the National Park Service in 1987 as a photographer at Grand Canyon National Park. Since 1992, he has traveled from his home in Seattle to Australia, New Zealand, the Atlantic Provinces of Canada, and the deserts of the American Southwest.

A recipient of the World Press Photo's Picture of the Year award, **Tom Reese** works for the *Seattle Times* and specializes in environmental subjects.

Originally from Mount Vernon, Washington, **Steve Ringman** works for the *Seattle Times* and received its Newspaper Photographer of the Year award in both 1984 and 1986.

Dean Rutz has photographed three Olympic Games for the *Seattle Times*. Originally from Palatine, Illinois, he has lived in the Seattle area for more than 10 years.

Having earned a degree in communications from the University of Washington, **Mike Siegel** resides in Washington and works for the *Seattle Times*.

Specializing in sports and general news photography, **Harley Soltes** works for the *Seattle Times*.

As the owner of Michael Townsend Photography, **Michael Townsend** specializes in travel, nature, and cultural imagery photography from 46 states and 40 countries. With 88,000 original images on file, he has been published in *Newsweek*, *Atlantic Monthly*, *Money & Seattle*, and other publications.

With awards from the National Press Photographers Association, the Society of Professional Journalists, and the Society of Newspaper Design, **Betty Udesen** specializes in news photography for the *Seattle Times*.

Rochelle Wells specializes in black-and-white portraiture and fine art photography. She currently works for Strode-McGowan Photography and has lived in the Seattle area for 10 years.

Barry Wong specializes in photojournalism and photo-illustration for the *Seattle Times*. Originally from San Francisco, he has lived in the Seattle area for more than 20 years.

Originally from Portland, Oregon, **Andrea J. Wright** has won several awards and specializes in news and feature photography for the *Seattle Times*.

Other contributing organizations include the Museum of History and Industry. For additional information about the photographers with images in *Seattle: The Time Has Come*, please contact Towery Publishing.

Index of Profiles